COMPASSION IN COLOR: FRAMEWORKS FOR WORKPLACE WELLNESS

Pamela Buchanan, MD | Dr. LaTia Greer, PsyD |

Dr. Evisha Ford | Tateanna Foster, LCSW | Dr. Fatimah Turner | Jessica H. Leigh, LCSW

Book cover design by Alek

Dr. Evisha Ford, Publisher
Chicago, IL

Table of Contents

Foreword

Compassion in Color is a special book.

In a world dominated by patriarchy and white supremacy, women of color have been systematically undermined in every sector of our society. Despite sitting at the intersections of oppression, they have continued to embody the best of us. Against the backdrop of structural injustice, women of color have selflessly shared their wisdom with a world committed to silencing them. In this book, we have been gifted with the benefits of their treasured insights.

Unlike most books of this nature, *Compassion in Color* is rooted in the real world. As veteran practitioners working across a wide range of domains, the authors provide wonderfully thick descriptions of their respective professional contexts. In each chapter, we are presented with a sober and unflinching analysis of the institutional, political, social, and cultural dynamics that conspire against the possibility of workplace wellness. With each contribution, we are empowered to transform sites of trauma and violence into spaces of healing and joy.

Perhaps the most refreshing thing about this book is its accessibility. Despite the analytic rigor of the essays, the contributors do not use academic jargon as a crutch or a shield. Although each writer possesses powerful expertise, they are unafraid to share vulnerable personal stories. While they each hold an esteemed degree and lofty title, the authors never fail to reveal their raw and unvarnished humanity.

Ultimately, this book is a book about wounded healing. Like the Greek god Chiron, the women in this text have been harmed by the violent force of institutional racism, sexism, and personal trauma. But, to the regret of our open enemies, they have refused to die. Instead, they have courageously struggled to heal their own wounds while navigating careers that are committed to leaving the world better than they found it. They have transformed their pain into power. And the world is better for it.

Now, in *Compassion in Color*, they have taught us how to follow their lead.

Read this beautiful book and prepare to be charged, challenged, and changed forever.

Marc Lamont Hill

1 | Pamela Buchanan, MD

Emerald Awakening: From Emotional Flatline to Revival

The Heartbeat of a Calling

The steady beep of the cardiac monitor once set the rhythm of my passion. Each peak and valley on that glowing green screen represented a life I could potentially save—a testament to the resilience of the human heart. As an emergency room (ER) doctor, I dreaded the moments when a flatline would suddenly spike, the shrill alarm piercing through the hushed tension of the room. Every doctor and nurse flinched at the sound, then silence would fall as the weight of another lost life piled heavily on our hearts.

After more than ten years of working as an ER doctor, my emotional health began to plateau. The peaks of exhilaration and valleys of compassion had given way to a monotonous, unbroken line of numbness.

Then COVID-19 hit.

The Onset of Burnout

Burnout is a slow, insidious process—more akin to heart failure than a heart attack. For me, it started before COVID and began with the little things. The twelve-hour shifts escalated to fourteen, then sixteen. The harsh fluorescent lights of the ER began to blur into one continuous glare. Sleep became a luxury, real meals a distant memory. The acrid taste of vending machine coffee substituted for the four main food groups, masking the metallic tang of exhaustion on my tongue.

Next, self-doubt, a common symptom of burnout, crept in, followed by constant second guessing. Each decision, even routine ones I'd made countless times before, now felt weighted with uncertainty. The once-comforting feel of my stethoscope started to feel like a noose.

I couldn't stop thinking about home. I was losing out on priceless family moments that I could never relive. I missed games, PTA meetings, everything. When my daughter's senior tennis night came and went without me, she said, "It's okay, Mom," her voice tinged with the disappointment she tried to hide. "I know your work is important." Those words stung more than any rebuke. I knew it wasn't okay, and I'd spend the rest of my life making it up to her.

Instead of addressing the issues, I dismissed the thoughts and feelings, convincing myself that they were a normal part of the life of an ER doctor. But, like a patient ignoring the warning signs of heart disease, I was setting myself up for a crisis. Little did I know that a global crisis was just around the corner.

Overwhelmed by the Pandemic

The COVID-19 pandemic hit the medical community like a massive heart attack. Just as a myocardial infarction cuts off blood flow to the heart, causing widespread damage, the pandemic abruptly overwhelmed healthcare systems, leaving medical professionals struggling to cope with the sudden influx of critically ill patients.

The ER transformed into a warzone, the air thick with fear and the sharp, bitter, and artificial smell of disinfectant. I felt like a soldier on the battlefield who was running out of ammunition. The weight of my quarantine protection gear—the N95 respirator, face shield, boot covers, hood, and gloves—was heavy but offered little protection against the enemy.

I was already struggling with burnout, working until exhaustion blurred my vision, my passion, and my own desire to live. On top of that, I had to watch helplessly as hundreds of lives slipped away. The rhythmic hiss of ventilators became a mocking chorus, punctuated by the ominous beep of faltering vitals. Each flatline on the monitor felt like a personal failure, a stark reminder of man's limitations.

The death toll became too much to bear. I had never encountered so much suffering. Just as a severe heart attack can leave permanent damage to the heart muscle, the relentless onslaught of COVID-19 was leaving deep scars on the psyche of healthcare workers, myself included.

One night, after losing two patients in a single shift, I retreated to my call room. The silence was a stark contrast to the ER's constant cacophony. I broke down, tears streaming down my face. The full weight of everything hit me, crushing my chest and making it difficult for me to breathe; it was a panic attack. I felt utterly useless, a fraud in a white coat. The passion that once drove me to medicine had flatlined completely.

I'd always been someone who could handle stress, or at least that's what I told myself. I'd been through a lot in my life, and I always found a way to keep moving forward. But the pandemic changed everything. It wasn't just the fear of the virus or the exhaustion from the long hours—it was the isolation. Despite the world coming to a halt and everyone staying at home, I remained an "essential worker." That meant I had no choice but to keep showing up, even when I felt like I couldn't anymore.

I experienced a level of isolation from my family that I had never experienced before. I was unable to spend time with my children in the way I desired. To mitigate the risk of exposing them to COVID, I had moved into the room above our garage, keeping my distance but yearning for a hug.

Every day, I stripped down in the garage to take a shower. I would hear them in the house, but I couldn't touch them, couldn't sit with them, breathe around them, and couldn't be the mom they needed and I wanted to be. My son, who has Crohn's disease, was on immunosuppressants, and the fear of passing the virus to him constantly stayed on my mind. The thought of hurting him and bringing this deadly virus into my home was unbearable, so I remained isolated. But staying away was making my depression worse.

Driving to work through empty streets was a strange experience. It felt like a ghost town, like one of those post-apocalyptic movies where everything looks abandoned but still, you scan the horizon hoping to see the silhouette of someone, anyone. The absence of typical traffic and the bustle of people going about their daily lives left me with nothing to divert my attention from the escalating darkness within my mind.

The Bridge Moment

To get to work, I drive over a steel suspension bridge that crosses the Missouri River. During the pandemic, that bridge became a symbol of my internal battle. Every time I crossed it, the same thought struck me: Jump.

The image was so vivid. I could see myself pulling over, parking the car, getting out, walking to the edge, and jumping into the river below. No hesitation at all. No one to yell for me to stop or overpower me just as I begin to fall forward. And for some reason, I always jumped from the right side of the bridge. It was as if I was watching myself from outside my body. I felt detached, but also so real.

At first, I told myself that the thoughts were due to exhaustion.

"You're tired," I'd say, shaking it off. "This is just stress-talking."

But the truth was, those thoughts weren't going away. In fact, they were getting louder. I found myself thinking about it every day, planning it in my mind.

It took every bit of force to drive to the other side of that bridge, make it to the hospital, and finish my shifts. But it was becoming harder to talk myself out of doing it.

So for months, I'd drive home, the monotonous hum of the road hypnotic, wondering what would happen if I just... didn't turn the steering wheel at the next curve. These thoughts were escalating and it terrified me, but it wasn't as terrifying as the fact that a part of me found it tempting.

A Glimmer of Hope

One evening, towards the end of my shift, my emergency department (ED) director came to relieve me. He had always been understanding, but that day, without knowing anything specific about my struggle, he said something that stuck with me.

"I know it's been hard," he said gently, his eyes crinkling with empathy above his mask. "But it will get better."

Those simple words, offered without prompting, provided an unexpected comfort. It was as if he had sensed the weight I was carrying. In that small statement, I found a glimmer of hope—the first tiny spark on my flatlined emotional cardiogram.

The Reality of Burnout

The World Health Organization explains that occupational burnout is the result of unaddressed chronic workplace stress, and it manifests in three key ways: emotional exhaustion, depersonalization (such as treating patients as objects rather than people), and a decreased sense of personal accomplishment.[1] I hit the trifecta.

Unfortunately, the journey to burnout was not unique to me. A 2019 National Physicians Survey found that 44% of physicians reported feeling burnout, with emergency medicine ranking among the top specialties.[2] But during the pandemic, burnout

---

[1] World Health Organization: WHO. (2019, May 28). Burn-out an "occupational phenomenon": International Classification of Diseases. *International Classification of Diseases (ICD-11)*.

[2] *Physician burnout in 2019, charted.* (2019, January 18). https://www.advisory.com/daily-briefing/2019/01/18/burnout-report

increased to an all-time high of 63%, according to the American Medical Association.[3]

Seeking Help

Admitting I needed help was the first step. I called therapist after therapist, my fingers trembling as I dialed each number. But my search for help wasn't as simple as booking an appointment with the assistant or completing an online form. I was facing waitlists, rejections, and insurance complications. When I finally found someone who could see me, a new fear gripped me, tightening my chest: What if she judged me? What if this impacted my career? I was terrified of losing my license and livelihood. However, my fear of losing my life outweighed all other fears, which was why I made the appointment.

In that first session, I hesitated speaking, the ticking of the clock on the wall marking each second of silence. Then I shared the reality of working in a rural Missouri ER, including the racial abuse I endured—

---

[3] American Medical Association & American Medical Association. (2022, September 15). Pandemic pushes U.S. doctor burnout to all-time high of 63%. *American Medical Association.* https://www.ama-assn.org/practice-management/physician-health/pandemic-pushes-us-doctor-burnout-all-time-high-63

the slurs that stung like physical blows. I had grown accustomed to colleagues assuming I was a nurse or support staff, patients questioning my credentials, or the palpable surprise when I demonstrated expertise in complex procedures. But during the pandemic, the frequency of racial slurs hurled my way increased alarmingly. "I've never been called a nigger more in my life than in those few years of the pandemic,"

The interactions had left me guarded and on edge in addition to dealing with the daily challenges of being an ER doctor. I was apprehensive about the reception of my honesty, yet I understood that facing these truths was necessary for my healing.

The B.E.A.T. Framework

Through therapy and self-reflection, I began to rebuild. It wasn't just random changes but a structured approach to recovery that guided me. As I sat in my therapist's office, the leather chair creaking softly beneath me, I could smell the faint aroma of lavender from the diffuser in the corner. Over the days, the gentle ticking of the wall clock marked the passage of time as I pieced together the elements crucial to my recovery. I call it B.E.A.T.— Balance, Empathy, Advocacy, and Transformation.

Balance

Burnout begins when we lose balance. In our training as doctors, we prioritize the needs of others over our own. However, I discovered the necessity of prioritizing my own well-being before tending to others.

To reclaim balance:

- I set firm boundaries at work, feeling the weight lift off my shoulders as I learned to say "no" to that extra shift.
- I scheduled non-negotiable time for activities that nourished both my body and mind. I savored the warmth of sunlight on my skin during midday walks and relished the burn in my muscles after a yoga session.
- I made self-care and time with loved ones protected time, non-negotiable parts of my routine. Exercise, mindfulness, and the laughter of my family during dinner became the sweetest sound, drowning out the echoes of hospital alarms in my mind.

Empathy

Empathy is both a strength and a vulnerability for healthcare providers. It can drive us to care for patients but also leave us drained. I had to learn to extend empathy to myself.

To cultivate self-empathy:

- I practiced daily self-compassion exercises. I felt the pen glide across paper as I wrote kind words to myself in my journal.
- I allocated 5 minutes after each shift to acknowledge my emotions without judgment, closing my eyes and feeling the rise and fall of my chest with each breath. Therapy gave me permission to feel what I was feeling and to accept that struggling didn't make me weak; it made me human.
- I confronted the emotional toll of my work and started to heal.

Advocacy

Advocacy for me was about pushing for systemic changes in healthcare that support the mental well-being of providers. Through this journey, I realized that I wasn't the only one who wanted change.

To advocate for change:

- I began speaking openly about my experience, my voice growing stronger with each retelling.
- I pushed for mental health resources for healthcare professionals, feeling a sense of purpose as I presented proposals to hospital administration.
- I encouraged others to seek help and push for a culture where it's okay to admit when we are not okay. The relief in a colleague's eyes when I shared my story was palpable, a silent acknowledgment of shared struggles.

Transformation

Transformation is the ongoing process of growth. I learned that healing isn't about returning to who I was; it's about evolving into a stronger, more self-aware version of myself.

To embrace transformation:

- I let go of perfectionism, feeling the tension release from my shoulders as I accepted that my best was enough.
- I established boundaries, and with practice, saying a firm "no" became easier.
- I reconnected with the passion that drew me to medicine in the first place. The first time I felt genuine joy while treating a patient again, it was like a warm current flowing through my veins, reminding me why I chose this path.

Revive Your Rhythm

In the field of medicine, we understand that a plateau is not the final outcome. With the right interventions, with care and persistence, we can restore a healthy rhythm. The B.E.A.T. framework is a call to "Revive Your Rhythm"—to find balance, practice self-empathy, advocate for change, and embrace transformation. The journey is not easy, but it is necessary.

To my fellow helping professionals, especially those who are struggling: I see you. I know the burdens you carry. Few people can truly comprehend the weight of life-and-death decisions, the long hours that stretch into days, and the emotional strain of witnessing daily suffering. But I want you to know that seeking help doesn't make you weak; it makes you human. It takes immense strength to admit when we're struggling and to reach out for support. By taking care of ourselves, we become better equipped to care for our patients. Only by nurturing our whole selves—physical, mental, spiritual, and emotional—can we truly fulfill the oaths and declarations of our professions.

And to the public: I implore you to remember that behind every white coat is a person doing their best in often impossible situations. We are not infallible machines, but human beings who feel deeply and care profoundly. We celebrate your triumphs and mourn your losses alongside you. We make decisions and provide care based on years of training, experience, and humanity. We face immense pressure, not just from the nature of our work but from a system that often prioritizes efficiency over empathy. When you or your loved ones interact with healthcare providers, please remember that we're navigating complex challenges, often with limited resources and time. Your understanding, patience, and kindness can make a world of difference in our day. By fostering mutual respect and empathy between healthcare providers and the public, we can create a more compassionate and effective healthcare system for everyone.

A New Rhythm

Today, my emotional cardiogram shows a healthier rhythm. There will always be peaks and valleys in life due to the challenges it presents, but the flatline of burnout has taught me the importance of balance. By following the B.E.A.T. framework, I have restored a healthier, more sustainable rhythm in my life.

As I make my way across the ER now, my steps are purposeful. The familiar sounds and smells no longer overwhelm me but remind me of the important work I do. I feel the cool plastic of my stethoscope around my neck, no longer a burden but a tool of healing. The lightness in my heart balances the weight of my responsibility. I'm Dr. Buchanan, an ER physician, and my heart beats with renewed purpose.

Pamela Buchanan, MD

Dr. Pamela Buchanan is a board-certified physician with over 20 years of experience in private practice and emergency medicine.

A TEDx speaker and ambassador for the Lorna Beene Foundation, she is also the author of *Emotional Flatline* and a contributor to the anthology *Triumph in the Trenches: Navigating Success for Black Professionals Volume 2*.

Dr. Buchanan earned her undergraduate degree from Washington University and went on to study at Ross University School of Medicine. She completed her residency at Mercy Hospital in St. Louis, Missouri, where she has lived her entire life.

Known for her effortless connection with people, she takes great pride in understanding her patients. A mother of three, she enjoys traveling and reading in her spare time.

2 | Dr. LaTia Greer

Purple Reign: Leading with Wellness and Strength for Women of Color

The Power of Purple

Purple is more than my favorite color—it's a symbol of power, resilience, and regality. Historically associated with royalty, nobility, and wisdom, it represents the strength and dignity that Black women carry, often silently. For me, purple signifies reclaiming my personal power and honoring myself as a leader and a woman of color. This chapter is about embracing both vulnerability and power while navigating the chaos of the world. "Purple reign" is about showing up fully for ourselves through intentional self-care and leadership, recognizing that we are both strong and human. To lead effectively, we must first be well.

As a Black woman, licensed clinician, certified clinical trauma professional, and integrative mental health expert, I've learned that leadership isn't about losing ourselves in service to others—it's about finding our own balance. The color purple has guided me in reclaiming my wellness, reminding me that I am in control of my life when I prioritize my well-being, and I am in leadership when I empower others by doing the same. Together, let's explore how wellness and leadership can coexist and help us thrive in a world filled with challenges.

The Black Woman's Balancing Act

Let's be real for a moment. Being a Black woman often feels like walking through life with an invisible cape, placed on us by society's expectations for us to bear the weight of our personal trauma, societal pressures, and systemic racism, all while serving others. Trying to be everything to everybody at all times. And that's on top of the everyday stress of balancing work, family, and personal life. Truth is: The cape can be heavy. And when you combine a career in mental health leadership, you've got yourself a recipe for burnout with a side of imposter syndrome.

But here's the kicker: we're not just dealing with our own stuff. We're also helping our clients navigate their trauma. It's like being a therapist and a client at the same time—talk about mind-blowing experiences. This dual role, as exhausting as it can be, also gives us a unique perspective. We're not just talking the talk; we're walking the walk. And sometimes that walk looks more like a trip, stumble and a fall.

In my work as a mental health professional, I see it daily: Black women bearing the weight of the world while helping others heal. We support our clients through their trauma while simultaneously dealing with our own. It's exhausting, but it's also an opportunity to lead with vulnerability. I vividly recall the moment when I realized I was overwhelmed by expectations. I was nodding at my client during a therapy session when my inner voice screamed, "Girl, you need therapy, too!" That's when I realized we can't pour from an empty cup, especially when the cup is chipped from years of people pleasing and not tending to my own needs.

The first step to healing the world is acknowledging our own need for healing—taking off the cape and embracing our vulnerability. Purple reign is not about perfection; it's about showing up authentically, even when the world tells us we "have to" be strong at all times.

No is a Complete Sentence (and Sometimes a Lifesaver)

Remember the days when we thought being available 24/7 was a sign of dedication? Pure insanity, right? Boundaries are more than just saying no to late-night calls—they're about protecting your time, energy, and peace. This applies to both your personal and professional spheres.

Let me tell you about the time I learned the hard way that boundaries aren't just important—they're essential. As a Black woman who has faced many challenges and obstacles, this was easy, and I thought I could handle it all. I prided myself on being available, always ready to help, and always saying yes. It was my way of proving my dedication, of showing I could thrive in a demanding field.

But here's the thing about constantly saying yes: it's a fast track to burnout.

I remember the day my wake-up call came, quite literally. For weeks, I had been working tirelessly, taking on additional clients, staying late at the office, and responding to emails at all hours of the night. I was so overextended that one morning, I found myself rushing to a therapy session still in my pajamas.

Yes, you read that right. I, a mental health professional mental health expert, showed up to a client session in my sleepwear.

I couldn't help but notice the irony as I sat there, trying to maintain my composure despite being dressed for a pajama party. I was supposed to be helping others maintain their mental health, and I couldn't even manage to dress myself properly. It was embarrassing, unprofessional, and a glaring sign that something had to change.

That pajama incident became my turning point. It made me realize that by trying to be everything to everyone, I was short-changing myself and, potentially, my clients. I wasn't practicing what I preached about self-care and boundaries.

From that day forward, I made a commitment to myself. I learned to say no—to others and to personal overextensions. I started setting clear boundaries with clients, colleagues, and even family members. I allocated time for self-care and rest, and I appropriately attired myself even though I work from home.

This experience taught me that as Black women in leadership roles, especially in mental health, we often feel pressure to be superheroes. But the truth is, even superheroes need rest. Exhaustion hinders our ability to lead effectively.

So, to all my fellow Black women leaders out there: remember that "no" is not just a complete sentence; it's sometimes the most self-loving thing you can say. Your time, your energy, and your mental health are precious resources. Guard them fiercely. And if you ever find yourself debating whether to show up to work in pajamas or not show up at all, take it from me: it's time to reassess those boundaries.

Learning to say no might just save your career, your sanity, and yes, your professional wardrobe choices. Trust me, I've been there, and the view is much better from the other side—fully dressed and well-rested.

As Black women, we've often been taught to be everything to everyone, but reclaiming our wellness means valuing our "yes" and giving it intentionally. Boundaries are an essential part of reigning over our lives and leadership.

Listening When Your Body Says Enough

By setting boundaries, understanding our needs, and regularly reflecting on our wellness practices, we can protect our energy and lead with compassion. However, it's not enough to simply know these principles; we must also actively listen to the signals our bodies and minds give us. This brings us to a crucial component of leadership and self-care: the mind-body connection.

Our bodies have a way of letting us know when we've pushed too far. Headaches, fatigue, and that all-too-familiar eye twitch are signals that we are overextending ourselves. Stress doesn't simply reside in our thoughts; it invades our physical health. I remember a particularly stressful week when my to-do list alone triggered heart palpitations—my body was screaming for attention, and I finally had to listen. As leaders, we're often effective at advising others about self-care, but how often do we practice what we preach? Mindfulness, meditation, and yoga aren't just wellness trends—they are essential tools for staying balanced. Recognizing and honoring these signals isn't a sign of weakness; it's a powerful act of self-awareness and strength.

The Leadership and Wellness Framework for Women of Color

Let's explore the PURPLE Reign framework, a leadership and wellness model uniquely tailored for women of color. Each letter in PURPLE represents key aspects of sustaining personal well-being while leading with intention, care, and purpose. Designed to help leaders honor themselves as they serve others, this framework is a holistic guide. It emphasizes maintaining strength through balance, reflection, and self-awareness, reminding us that prioritizing wellness is not a luxury—it's essential for sustained leadership.

Prioritize Personal Boundaries

Leadership requires setting clear boundaries to maintain balance. This means identifying when to say "no" to overcommitment and protecting your time, energy, and emotional well-being. Healthy boundaries support emotional, occupational, and physical wellness by ensuring that you have space for rest, reflection, and self-care.

Understand Your Needs

Understanding your personal wellness needs across the eight dimensions (physical, emotional, intellectual, social, spiritual, occupational, financial, and environmental) is key to thriving as a leader. This involves self-awareness and continuous reflection on what helps you maintain balance and what drains you. It's about tuning in to your body, emotions, and energy levels, allowing you to take proactive steps toward self-care and prevent burnout.

Reflect on Wellness Practices

Regularly reflect on your wellness routines and how they align with your leadership role. This could include mindfulness practices, journaling, exercise, or other forms of self-care. Reflection helps you stay grounded, assess your progress, and adjust your practices to ensure they support all areas of your wellness, from spiritual to financial well-being.

Protect Your Energy

Leadership can be demanding, especially for women of color who may face additional cultural and systemic pressures. Protecting your energy requires choosing who and what to focus on. It's about recognizing what energizes and drains you, allowing you to make conscious choices to engage in activities that align with your values and wellness goals. This also ties into emotional and social wellness by fostering positive, supportive relationships.

Lead with Self-Compassion

As a leader, showing compassion to yourself is crucial. This means accepting that you're not perfect, taking breaks, and asking for help. Self-compassion builds resilience and supports emotional wellness, helping you manage stress and setbacks with grace and allowing you to show up authentically in your leadership roles.

Empowering your well-being means taking ownership of your wellness journey and being proactive in nurturing the eight domains of well-being. This could involve setting financial goals, creating a peaceful home environment, or seeking professional development opportunities. As you empower yourself, you also become a model of balanced leadership for others, demonstrating that well-being is integral to effective leadership, not a secondary priority.

"REIGN" compliments the framework and speaks directly to the leadership journeys of Black women. We're not just leading in traditional ways; we're leading with resilience, empowerment, growth, and grounded wellness at the center. We embrace boundaries as acts of self-preservation and thrive by honoring ourselves while lifting others.

Resilience is not about pushing until we break—it's about understanding the strength in pacing ourselves and practicing self-care. Empowerment means leading by creating spaces where others can grow. Inspiring growth reflects the continuous evolution of our emotional, spiritual, and mental well-being. Grounded in wellness, we can lead without exhaustion, maintaining wholeness across the eight dimensions of wellness. Navigating boundaries ensures we protect our energy and lead with clarity and compassion. Through this framework, we reign by nurturing ourselves as much as those we lead, standing strong in our leadership while prioritizing intentional care, balance, and growth. Purple reign isn't just a color; it's the embodiment of powerful, purposeful leadership for women of color.

The 8 Dimensions of Wellness

Wellness isn't about perfection; it's about balance. Achieving balance in leadership requires nurturing all aspects of our well-being, which is why the eight domains of wellness are so critical. Tending to these interconnected domains—emotional, physical, social, occupational, spiritual, intellectual, environmental, and financial—holistically is key to thriving.[4] Let's explore how each of these dimensions plays a role in maintaining that balance.

Emotional Wellness

Therapy isn't just for clients. It's essential to process our own emotions. Journaling, venting to a friend, or even screaming into a pillow (no judgment) are all valid ways to care for your emotional health.

Physical Wellness

Taking care of your body is a form of self-respect. Netflix and wine have their place, but so do regular movement and sleep. Sleep is sacred—protect it.

Social Wellness

Lean into your support system. The quality of your relationships is more important than quantity. Find your circle of trust, whether it's close friends or community.

---

[4] *Mapping Mental Health: Dr. Swarbrick & the Eight Wellness Dimensions | Center of Alcohol & Substance Use Studies.* (n.d.). https://alcoholstudies.rutgers.edu/mapping-mental-health-dr-swarbrick-the-eight-wellness-dimensions/.

Occupational Wellness

You don't have to do it all. Delegate. Setting boundaries at work and modeling work-life balance benefits everyone on your team.

Spiritual Wellness

Find what centers you, whether it's religion, mindfulness, or nature. Spiritual wellness keeps you grounded in something bigger than yourself.

Intellectual Wellness

Never stop learning. Growth is about intellectual stimulation—whether it's through reading, podcasts, or discussions that challenge your thinking.

Environmental Wellness

Your surroundings matter. A cluttered space can lead to a cluttered mind. Create an environment that promotes peace and clarity.

Financial Wellness

Money may not buy happiness, but it reduces stress. Managing your finances with intention gives you security and freedom.

Reign Over Your Wellness

To every woman of color reading this: it's time to embrace your reign. With wellness as your foundation, you have the power to lead not only in your career but also in your life. Here's how you can take action today:

Reclaim Your Time

Set one boundary this week that protects your mental or emotional health. Whether it's saying no to an extra responsibility or carving out time for yourself, make it a priority.

Invest in Your Wellness

Choose one and more of the eight dimensions of wellness that need attention in your life. Whether it's physical, financial, or emotional, take a small step toward nurturing that area today.

Check in with Yourself

Schedule time to assess your own wellness—whether it's through journaling, a self-care day, or even a mental health check-in with a professional. Your wellness matters as much as your clients' or your team's.

Support Other Women of Color

Lift as you climb. By sharing your journey, demonstrating balanced leadership, and fostering environments that prioritize wellness, you can empower others.

Your reign is waiting. Step into it with confidence, compassion, and the understanding that true power lies in prioritizing your own well-being. The time to reign with wellness and strength is now—lead with purple, lead with purpose.

Purple Reign and Beyond

As Black women in leadership, we embody the essence of purple: regal, resilient, and empowered. Our leadership isn't just about leading others; it's about leading ourselves with grace, compassion, and wellness at the forefront. "Purple reign."

Dr. LaTia Greer

Meet Dr. LaTia Greer, a dynamic voice in the chorus of healing and transformation, whose story interweaves with others in a powerful testament to mental wellness and personal growth.

As a Licensed Clinical Professional Counselor and Certified Integrative Mental Health Professional, Dr. Greer brings her unique perspective to this collaborative anthology. Her contribution isn't just professional wisdom—it's a heartfelt invitation to explore the intersection of mental health, storytelling, and communal healing.

What sets her apart? It's her genuine belief that every voice deserves to be heard, especially within the Black community where mental health conversations often happen in whispers. Through her chapter, she joins fellow authors in breaking down barriers and building bridges, creating space for authentic dialogue about mental wellness.

When she's not counseling or contributing to groundbreaking anthologies, Dr. Greer finds her own path to wellness through nature walks, mindfulness practices, and the occasional glass of wine—proving that mental health professionals are human too, embracing both the work and joy of self-care.

In this collaborative work, Dr. Greer stands alongside other powerful voices, each sharing their unique perspective on mental health, resilience, and personal transformation. Her contribution adds a vital thread to this tapestry of experiences, particularly in supporting Black women and families on their journey to emotional wellness.

Join Dr. Greer and her fellow authors as they weave together stories of challenge, triumph, and everything in between. Because sometimes the most powerful healing happens when we realize we're not alone in our journey.

Ready to discover the strength in shared stories? Turn the page—your own journey of discovery awaits.

3 | Dr. Evisha Ford

Ambition is the New **Black**: Creating Compassionate Work Environments for POC

As I stumbled into my office, exhaustion weighing heavily on my shoulders, tears streamed down my cheeks, a silent testament to the battles fought within. My therapist's words echoed in my mind like a mantra: "If you're okay, your boys will be okay." Each morning, I poured every ounce of my being into crafting a façade of normalcy, clinging to the hope that somehow it would be enough...

During this season, I was bearing the crushing weight of a pending divorce. My heart was heavy, and every day felt like a fight. I stepped into the ring of what had become my life, taking each gut punch for my children's survival. Despite my efforts to maintain a tidy facade, the signs of stress began to show. I started losing weight (a welcome loss), struggled to focus on tasks, and spent a great deal of time avoiding contact with people to whom I had to give an account. In hindsight, it was clear that anyone paying attention could see my struggle.

Fortunately, I chose to openly discuss the state of affairs (pun intended!) between my then-husband and me with my direct supervisor. Not only had I known my supervisor for more than a decade, but he was also wise and could keep a secret like no other. I also shared this information with him as a matter of practicality. I thought it might be advantageous to explain why my eyes were bloodshot in the mornings and why I often needed a closed door to start my day. Most importantly, I shared this information because I sensed his genuine concern.

I often wondered if the grace I received during this difficult season was an anomaly. I happened to know of three other colleagues—all women in leadership within the same organization—who were experiencing similar trials. They couldn't hide their struggle from me because it's difficult to elude people living inside the same nightmare. Two of the three women reported to me, so I did what I could without being intrusive—offered a kind word, extended extra grace, and attempted to be present—paying forward the kindness that was extended to me.

This season laid a foundational stone for me. Despite spending more than ten years in executive leadership, this was the first time "life" struck me with such force. In another work environment, I might have taken leave because, for the first time, I couldn't rely on my work ethic, critical thinking, or experience. It was clear that I was beholden to the compassion of others. This experience set the tone for my leadership; I committed to always offer that gift to others.

I knew instinctively that compassion was rarely available in the workplace, especially for people of color. Tamara Beauboeuf-Lafontant asserts, "Black women's...experiences continue to be shaped by a legacy of neglect...The pain of Black women is often minimized or dismissed, perpetuating a cycle of invisibility and invalidation."[5] Many organizations only value people for their contributions to the bottom line, discarding them when they fail to produce. I vowed never to ask people of color to "work harder" in a system not designed for their success. I chose to foster a space within my own organization that created every opportunity for all people to succeed.

In the nuanced corridors of professional life, where the hum of productivity masks the deeper undercurrents, people of color (POC) often navigate a terrain laden with unspoken challenges. Often overlooked in the broader discourse, the impact of work environments on POC is characterized by a unique blend of resilience and strain. Understanding how trauma manifests in these spaces—sometimes subtly, sometimes starkly—is essential for fostering workplaces that are not just inclusive but also genuinely supportive.

Trauma in the workplace isn't always the result of overt incidents; it often stems from the cumulative

---

[5] Tamara Beauboeuf-Lafontant, Behind the Mask of the Strong Black Woman: Voice and the Embodiment of a Costly Performance. Temple University Press, 2009.

weight of microaggressions, systemic inequities, and the constant negotiation of identity. For POC, the workplace can become a battlefield, where the fight isn't just for professional recognition but for psychological safety. The scars left by these daily battles are often invisible, yet they run deep, affecting not just individual performance but also collective well-being.

This chapter delves into the principles of trauma-compassionate leadership—an approach that recognizes hidden struggles and seeks to address them with empathy, awareness, and action. Through compelling case studies, we will explore how leaders who embrace these principles can transform workplaces from spaces of silent strain to environments of healing and growth.

Finally, this chapter provides actionable steps for leaders who are committed to fostering an equitable and supportive workplace. It also provides insight for mental health providers who are often tasked to pick up the fragmented pieces left behind. By understanding trauma, embracing compassionate leadership, and implementing practical strategies, leaders can make a profound impact on the lives of their employees, particularly those from marginalized communities. The journey begins with awareness, but it culminates in the tangible actions that create truly inclusive and thriving work environments.

Impact of Work Environment on POC

We spend a great deal of time at work. There is no doubt that the work environment profoundly impacts well-being, encompassing mental, emotional, and physical health. A supportive and positive workplace fosters a sense of belonging, reduces stress, and enhances job satisfaction, contributing to overall well-being, which is what I experienced in the most difficult of seasons.[6] Conversely, a toxic work environment can lead to increased stress, burnout, and a decline in both mental and physical health, which I can also attest to from firsthand experience.

---

[6] Nielsen, K., & Einarsen, S. (2018). What are the risk factors for workplace bullying? *Work & Stress, 32*(2), 105-119. doi:10.1080/02678373.2018.1457735.

Before transitioning into leadership, I spent several years working with vulnerable populations. After earning my MSW, I thought my career would remain centered on domestic violence, but I became deeply interested in the plight of children living in shelters. My clinical experience expanded as I worked with homeless youth struggling with anxiety, trauma—emerging as a phenomenon at that time—and youth exiting the sex trade industry. It was here that I learned my first lesson: "person in environment," the cornerstone of social work that considers how a person's environment affects their behavior and well-being.[7]

The realization that stuck with me was that all these individuals—homeless teens, children in shelters, youth sex workers—had one thing in common: they all attended school. This insight led me into school social work and, eventually, to leadership in the field. I learned early on that the learning environment matters profoundly for youth. As my career

---

[7] Social Work Test Prep. (2023, May 15). Person-in-Environment (PIE) Theory (ASWB Exam Content Spotlight). *Social Work Test Prep.* https://socialworktestprep.com/blog/2022/december/23/person-in-environment-pie-theory-aswb-exam-content-spotlight/?srsltid=AfmBOooG4fEOSRhSrcarXkqwydo8TdyFbH8QMcbfHxamYQ9Dqg3brp29.

progressed, I saw this same principle applied to adults. The workplace, like the classroom, can either nurture or suppress a person's ability to thrive. For people of color, particularly, a work environment that fails to address systemic inequities or microaggressions can act as a barrier to both personal and professional growth. [8]

I can recall, as a young leader, being sent into a senior leadership team to announce shifts in a deeply entrenched, sacred process. There was an unspoken tension. Reflecting on it now, I realize that I was ill-prepared for such a task. I was new to the organization, had yet to establish meaningful connections, and lacked a comprehensive understanding of the change's ramifications. I was quite literally the only woman and person of color in a room full of dark suits and ties. Unfortunately, the superintendent, in either a gross miscalculation or blatant disregard, failed to anticipate the fury that would erupt.

---

[8] Smith, W. A., Allen, W. R., & Danley, L. L. (2019). "Assumed incompetent": Racial microaggressions and their mental health implications for Black professionals in the academy. *Journal of Negro Education*, 88(2), 125-138.

One of the board-protected organizational tyrants stood up and shouted in red-faced anger that I didn't know what I was talking about and that no such change would occur. At that moment, I was acutely aware of the organizational chart, which showed my position above his. Yet, this hierarchy did nothing to shield me from the wave of humiliation that streamed down my face, not just from the embarrassment but from the realization of my utter isolation. I glanced around the room, silently pleading for the superintendent, my supervisor, or anyone else to step in and support me. The deafening silence made it painfully clear that no one was helping me in that meeting or that day.

Had I looked like everyone else in the room—white or male—I cannot imagine that I would have faced such venomous fury. For people of color, the effects of a toxic workplace can be even more pronounced due to additional layers of stress, such as microaggressions, discrimination, and the constant pressure of having to prove oneself. The lack of representation and the feeling of being an outsider can exacerbate feelings of isolation and reduce the sense of belonging, making it harder to thrive in the workplace.

Inclusivity and diversity play crucial roles in improving workplace conditions. When organizations prioritize inclusivity, they create environments where everyone feels valued and respected, regardless of their background.[9] This sense of belonging can alleviate the unique stresses faced by people of color. Diversity brings a wealth of perspectives and ideas, fostering innovation and creativity. It challenges stereotypes and reduces biases, contributing to a more equitable work environment.

A toxic work environment can have severe and far-reaching effects on an individual's mental health. Constant exposure to negativity, such as bullying, harassment, unfair treatment, or relentless pressure, can lead to chronic stress, anxiety, and depression. Employees in these environments often experience a significant drop in self-esteem, feelings of helplessness, and a sense of worthlessness.

---

[9] Brown, B. (2020). *Dare to Lead: Brave Work. Tough Conversations. Whole Hearts.* Random House.

Over time, these stressors can contribute to a state of physical, emotional, and mental exhaustion. In extreme cases, individuals may develop symptoms of post-traumatic stress disorder (PTSD), particularly if the toxicity includes elements of abuse or severe harassment. Additionally, the emotional strain from a toxic work environment can spill over into personal life, affecting relationships, sleep patterns, and overall well-being. Mental health professionals absorb this "spillover" more frequently than compassionate leaders.

As a committed compassionate leader, I believe it is imperative to not only acknowledge the impact but also implement policies that promote equality, provide support systems, and foster a culture of empathy and understanding. By doing so, we not only improve the well-being of individuals but also enhance the overall productivity and success of the organization.

Understanding Trauma in the Workplace

"Why did you wait until now to dismiss her?" The question—sincere and vulnerable—pierced my heart. It came from a young leader I respected, a woman who has grown within the organization and whom I have grown to deeply admire. Her words reflected not just curiosity but also a profound need for reassurance—a need to understand her place and value within our team dynamics.

This question brought to light a more profound problem—her uncertainty about the value of her feedback. It became clear that someone had caused her to doubt the reliability of her intuition, planting a seed of self-doubt. I refused to nurture this seed. Instead, I committed to uprooting any personal or historical trauma that led this young, capable woman to question herself. My mission was to affirm her worth and ensure she never doubted her intuition again.[10]

---

[10] Neville, H. A., & Tynes, B. M. (2021). *Psychological Health of People of Color: Scientific and Practice Considerations*. American Psychological Association.

Complex trauma, stemming from prolonged exposure to harmful situations such as systemic discrimination, profoundly impacts self-perception and perceived value, especially in the workplace. Individuals who have endured complex trauma often struggle with feelings of worthlessness, inadequacy, and a pervasive sense of not belonging. These internalized negative beliefs shape how they view themselves and their contributions in a professional setting.[11]

Furthermore, complex trauma can result in heightened sensitivity to criticism and a tendency to internalize negative feedback more deeply than their peers. This can create a cycle of anxiety and stress, further eroding their confidence and reinforcing their negative self-perceptions. Regardless of their actual performance, these individuals may also struggle with imposter syndrome, feeling constantly on the verge of exposure as frauds, regardless of their actual performance.

---

[11] Williams, M. T. (2020). The link between racism and PTSD: Towards a culturally informed trauma model. *American Psychological Association*, 75(9), 927-936.

The young leader on my team, a woman of color, had meticulously crafted a remediation plan for an underperforming employee—let's call her Karen. The plan was comprehensive, detailing the steps Karen needed to take to improve her performance. Another team member, assigned to provide coaching, reported significant resistance from Karen on the very day we were required to review the plan.

Despite Karen's consistent underperformance, the situation required careful handling. We had a legal obligation to provide Karen with every opportunity to meet the outlined expectations. I prioritized following all protocols over waiting for feedback from others.

In a surprising twist, this young leader summoned the courage to question the timing of my decision. "Why did you wait until now to dismiss her?" Her challenge provided a crucial moment for me. I could have responded with ego and taken exception to being questioned. Instead, I seized the opportunity to not only clarify the importance of adhering to the remediation plan but, more significantly, to validate her intuition and leadership qualities.

I took this moment to dismantle the negative messages that the young woman had internalized. I needed to affirm her worth and capabilities and let her know that she was, indeed, an incredible and intuitive leader. This interaction was more than just a procedural necessity; it was an opportunity to empower and reinforce confidence.

In this exchange, I learned the power of listening and validating others, recognizing that leadership is as much about nurturing potential as it is about making tough decisions. This experience underscored the importance of empathy and support in fostering a truly inclusive and empowering workplace.

All people bring their previous experience into the workplace. To ensure the success of people of color, we must address these challenges by creating supportive and understanding environments.

Principles of a Trauma-Compassionate Workplace

One morning, I found myself caught between two worlds. One of my team members was compulsively texting me, seeking validation and support. My well-meaning girlfriend, noticing my distraction, became frustrated. "Girl, this is not your purpose," she said, exasperated and sympathetic that I wasn't fully present over our breakfast cocktails on Miami Beach.

What she didn't know was that the man on the other end of those texts was in a domestic violence situation. Our professional relationship had given me the insight I needed to understand the gravity of his predicament. To be clear, I would have preferred to enjoy our time together without interruption. But I knew that for a 6-foot tall, heterosexual man trapped in such a situation, finding a judgment-free, safe space to reach out was incredibly rare.

In that moment, I recognized that my role as a trauma-informed leader required me to be available and supportive, even when it was inconvenient. My commitment to providing a safe, affirming space couldn't be conditional. It had to be unwavering. This experience underscored the essence of trauma-informed practices—understanding the hidden struggles of those we lead and offering support without judgment when needed.

Throughout this chapter, I have referenced a trauma-informed approach in the workplace. Here is what that looks like in its most simple form, according to the Centers for Disease Control and Prevention (CDC):

Safety

Ensure physical and emotional safety for all employees. This involves creating a secure environment where individuals feel protected from harm. This aspect was not present in my experience as a young leader.

Trustworthiness and Transparency

Establish and maintain trust through open communication, consistency, and transparency in decision-making processes. I discussed my strategies for re-establishing trust with a team leader.

Peer Support

Foster a sense of community and mutual support among employees, encouraging peer-to-peer connections. The manner in which I sought opportunities to encourage other women who I knew were struggling is a great example of peer support.

Collaboration and Mutuality

Promote teamwork and shared decision-making, recognizing the value of everyone's contribution.

Empowerment, Voice, and Choice

Empower employees by providing them with options and respecting their autonomy and input.

Cultural, Historical, and Gender Issues

Address and be sensitive to cultural, historical, and gender-related factors that might impact individuals' experiences of trauma. As leaders, we must commit to an increased awareness of the lived experiences of those that we support, including people of color.[12]

I prefer to refer to "trauma-compassionate" approaches because they allow us to receive

---

[12] *Building Trauma-Informed Communities | Blogs | CDC.* (2022, May 25). https://blogs.cdc.gov/publichealthmatters/2022/05/trauma-informed/.

information without taking action. However, the definition of compassion denotes action.

Actionable Steps for Mental Health Professionals

Mental health professionals play a crucial role in helping individuals navigate the challenges posed by toxic workplaces—environments not marked by trauma-informed practices. Among the crucial ways they can provide support are the following approaches:

Create Safe Spaces

The first step is to provide a safe, non-judgmental space where the client feels heard and validated. Acknowledging their experiences and the impact of the toxic environment on their mental health is essential.

Develop Coping Strategies

Therapists can teach stress management techniques, such as mindfulness, relaxation exercises, and time management strategies, to help clients cope with the immediate effects of their work environment.

Career Alignment

For some clients, it may be helpful to explore whether their current job aligns with their personal values and long-term career goals. This can lead to discussions about potential career changes or other ways to seek fulfillment outside of a toxic work setting. This might involve job searching, financial planning, and mental preparation for leaving the toxic environment.

Referral to Additional Resources

In cases where the client's mental health is severely affected, a therapist might refer them to a psychiatrist for medication management or recommend other supportive services, such as legal advice, when workplace harassment or discrimination persists.

Framework for Trauma-Compassionate workplaces: HEAL

I wrote this chapter from the perspective of a trained mental health clinician, but over the past two decades, I have applied that training in my role as an executive leader. It would be remiss not to discuss the implementation of these principles by those in leadership roles, given the intrinsic link between clinical work and leadership. In this chapter, we explored the vital role leaders play in fostering a compassionate, trauma-informed workplace. Leaders have the responsibility to create environments where all employees feel safe, valued, and supported through practices grounded in humanity, empathy, awareness, and strong leadership.

Humanity: Acknowledge the Person Behind the Role

Leaders must see employees as whole individuals, not just as workers fulfilling tasks. This means acknowledging their life struggles, identities, and the unique burdens they carry, particularly for people of color navigating systemic inequities.

Empathy: Lead with Compassion

Empathy requires not only understanding but also acting to support others in difficult situations. For leaders, this means recognizing invisible battles (e.g., trauma, microaggressions) and being proactive in offering grace, support, and kindness.

Awareness: Understand the Impact of Trauma

Leaders need to understand how workplace trauma, particularly related to discrimination and systemic issues, manifests. This includes recognizing the toll of toxic environments, microaggressions, and the constant need for people of color to prove their worth.

Leadership: Create Policies and Culture of Equity

Leadership requires taking deliberate action to foster an equitable, trauma-compassionate workplace. This includes enacting policies that promote inclusivity, provide mental health support, and build a culture where everyone feels safe and valued.

The HEAL framework is a call for leaders to:

- Recognize and address hidden struggles in their teams.
- Lead with empathy, fostering an environment of compassion.
- Actively promote diversity, equity, and inclusion policies.
- Commit to ongoing learning and adaptation to meet the needs of all employees, particularly marginalized groups.

The next chapter will delve deeper into specific policy changes and organizational practices that can further enhance a trauma-informed workplace.

For leaders, continuous learning and self-reflection are crucial. Understanding the workplace experiences of people of color and the impact is an ongoing process. To better support their teams, leaders must commit to educating themselves, reflecting on their actions, and making necessary adjustments.

Leaders must also prioritize the well-being of their diverse workforce. By embracing trauma-informed practices, we can create workplaces where every individual feels seen, heard, and valued. Let us commit to building compassionate environments that promote healing, growth, and actual opportunity for all employees.

As we move forward, remember that this journey requires dedication, empathy, and a willingness to learn and adapt. Together, we can make a meaningful difference in the lives of those we serve.

Dr. Evisha Ford

Dr. Evisha Ford is a visionary leader and advocate for marginalized youth, driven by a passion that has shaped her entire career. As the Founding Executive Director of iCan Dream Center, a therapeutic school in Illinois, she is transforming the lives of neurodiverse learners and their families. Beginning her journey by supporting inner-city homeless youth in Chicago, Dr. Evisha provided critical therapeutic intervention and linked young people to vital community resources. Chicago Public Schools recruited her, solidifying her commitment to education and setting her on a path to leadership.

With a rich background as an Assistant Superintendent, Director of Special Education, and Assistant Professor of Educational Leadership, Dr. Evisha is a sought-after thought leader both nationally and internationally. She specializes in trauma-compassionate leadership, racial equity, and designing programs that empower diverse learners. As the author of Benches in the Bathroom: Leading a Physically, Emotionally, and Socially Safe School Culture, her insights have shaped conversations around effective school and nonprofit leadership. In 2024, she took the TEDx stage to share her message of compassionate leadership.

Dr. Evisha's academic foundation includes a Master of Social Work from the University of Illinois and a Doctorate in Educational Leadership from Aurora University. Her research focus was on emotional disabilities, youth resiliency, and critical race theory. Her contributions earned her the "Woman of the Year" award and recognition as one of the "100

Black Influential Women in Chicago." She has received numerous awards since that time. Her most generous acknowledgment as "the best," however, comes from her husband and two sons.

Dr. Evisha shares her expertise through her biweekly LinkedIn newsletter, Compassion Investors. To learn more about her impactful work, visit drevisha.com or follow her on LinkedIn.

4 | Tateanna Foster, LCSW

Removing the Red Tape: Bold Initiatives for Supporting Minority Mental Health

I remember being thirteen years old I spent all day playing outside at my cousin's house. When we walked in my mom told me it was time to go home. As I slowly gathered my belongings me and my cousin eavesdropped on a conversation between my mother and his. Naturally, as a child, we always wanted to be in the mix of what grown people were discussing. I remember the disdain both our parents shared about their jobs. My aunt spoke about her supervisor being snide and insensitive; my mother expressed dissatisfaction with her pay after being with the agency for eight years. I remember my cousin looking at me and whispering, "We're never working at places like that," and we laughed silently with each other. To my surprise, I would be hearing complaints like this throughout my adulthood from family members, friends, and colleagues. And despite the childhood oath made with my cousin, I would experience very similar circumstances in the workforce that would negatively contribute to my mental health.

Shoulders square, chin held high, we stride
Through corridors where shadows of bias reside
Our presence a testament, our voices a light
In this realm where wrongs yearn to be right
Our mind, impacted yet unbound and free
A testament to all we're meant to be
Change on the horizon, shifts render gleams

—Anna Tate

Work Wounds

Examining the mental health of minorities requires an honest look at how the workforce impacts the psychological well-being of BIPOC individuals. Ideally, people would wake up eager to contribute their skills in workplaces that affirm, support, and celebrate their unique contributions—not just for what they do but for who they are. Yet, the reality is often different: people of color frequently face disproportionately higher rates of mental health issues due to systemic racism, socioeconomic disparities, and traumatic exposures. These factors create a heavier mental load, compounded by workplace structures that are often indifferent or actively hostile to the well-being of minorities.

When I graduated with a Master's in Social Work in 2016, I was driven to address service gaps in underserved communities, particularly supporting teenage mothers. I joined a national organization, conducting weekly home visits and leading support groups that fostered connection and mutual support. Initially, I felt welcomed with a supervisor who showed genuine interest in my growth. But soon, her demeanor shifted—coldness, passive remarks about my age, and the unacknowledged weight of increased responsibilities strained our relationship. My mother's cancer diagnosis compounded this stress, and each morning, I would show up to work 15 minutes early to allow myself time to cry and pray before I walked into a space that no longer felt welcoming. I was struggling to control my "understudy."

This experience highlights the importance of addressing "work wounds"—the microaggressions, biased evaluations, and unequal treatment that many underrepresented groups face. I eventually overheard two coworkers discussing the pattern of treatment that was affecting me, and I realized I was the third person of color to hold my position, with others before me enduring similar experiences. Although I left the company, my story reflects the shared struggles many face in the workplace.

Currently, as a mental health consultant, I've facilitated many employees' mental health groups where similar experiences are shared. These individuals, from diverse backgrounds and identities, often tell stories of workplace mistreatment tied to their identities, leading to anxiety, depression, and distress. They routinely endure what I call "work wounds." These "work wounds" don't remain at work; they follow us home, affecting our emotions, our relationships, and our overall mental health. A common theme is the lack of safety or empowerment any of us felt to address these issues openly.

Given the immense time individuals spend at work—over a third of their day, according to the U.S. Bureau of Labor Statistics[13]—this environment plays a critical role in shaping their mental health. Unfortunately for human beings, no matter how hard we attempt, we cannot compartmentalize our mental health to just one environment that we experience. We can attempt to radiate main character energy, showing up as our best selves to navigate our workplace environment but unaddressed or addressed and unresolved concerns can and will trigger "the understudy." "The understudies" or our emotionally reactive selves, undermine our best intentions to navigate toxic work cultures. Everywhere you are, your mind will also be right alongside your emotions and the physiological effects of enduring a toxic atmosphere that stifles your well-being due to persistent negative experiences. Considering all these emotions, your

---

[13] U.S. Bureau of Labor Statistics. (2023, September 20). *American time use survey summary* (USDL-23-1804). https://www.bls.gov/news.release/pdf/atus.pdf.

understudy will be practicing their lines in the background, waiting for an opportunity to be the star.

Protective Practices

Keeping the understudy at bay requires building an arsenal of coping skills, but another essential tool is radical honesty and self-advocacy. However, we have to acknowledge that for employees to even feel close to comfortable confronting issues openly, the workplace must feel safe—a safety built through leadership intentionally cultivating strong relationships and protective practices that exemplify a commitment to actively support and advocate for minority team members. There is consistent evidence linking leadership in organizations to the psychological well-being of employees.

Supporting the mental health of minority employees can begin at the basis of understanding how enduring offenses such as microaggressions, income inequality, and unfair promotion processes, to name a few, can take a tremendous toll on the well-being of employees. I challenge companies to see certain issues that minorities deal with because of their identities as "wounds." Somewhere, it reads that "an offense is a wound, an injury to the soul." I will define a "work wound" as a situation a minority employee experiences in the workplace that ruptures their confidence in their counterpart's ability to demonstrate inclusivity and acceptance at a given time. How often are the psyches of minority employees injured because of unaddressed wounds? Whether the incident is unintentional or not is inconsequential. Companies can begin to heal work wounds when they orchestrate a safe space for employees to identify and process demoralizing behaviors.

I have created a Work Wound Reflection form to assist Human Resources or leaders in leading a restorative process when an employee experiences a "work wound." The employee will be given a Work Wound Reflection Form. This form is the initial step to a simplistic yet powerful approach to healing a "work wound." The form will set a foundation for reflection and accountability. The Work Wound Reflection Form empowers employees with succinct language that addresses the emotional and psychological effects workplace offenses can cause.

Example:

Describe the wound/offense:

How did the wound affect you internally and externally:

Internal:

- ☐ Dismissed
- ☐ Humiliation
- ☐ Disregarded
- ☐ Shut Down
- ☐ (Employee can insert additional)

External:

- ☐ Inability to focus
- ☐ Isolated from the team
- ☐ Stagnation in creativity
- ☐ Decreased confidence to share ideas
- ☐ (Employee can insert additional)

Was the wound open or closed:

Open:

The wound was exposed to the wounded and other team members. Explain:

Closed:

The wound was between the wounded and the person who inflicted the wound. Explain:

Was the wound acute or chronic:

Acute:

This is the first time the wound has occurred. Explain:

Chronic:

The wound is acknowledged to be a pattern of behavior. Explain:

Understanding the Process

The employee is first asked to describe what caused the wound or offense in detail. The employee will then take time to identify how the work wound was/is affecting them under two specific categories. The internal wound and the external wound they are experiencing. The internal effects deal directly with the employee's emotions. They can choose from examples given on the form or insert their own emotions that surface. The employee will also highlight the external wounds, which are factors that are now affecting the employee's ability to show up as their best selves. Additionally, the employee will reflect on whether this was an open or closed wound.

Simply put, an open work wound resulted in the exposure of the offense to other bystanders witnessing the wound. A closed wound is accounted for between the one who inflicted the wound and the wounded only. The last step is for the employee to express if this situation was an acute or chronic wound. A chronic offense represents behavior that an employee can express as a noted pattern or a repeated pattern. An acute work wound is an offense that employees acknowledge to date is a one-time offense. Upon completion of the form, the employee has the option to address the person who inflicted the wound with support or to accept completing the form as a cathartic release.

Accountability

When an employee chooses to address the "work wound" with the leader who inflicted the wound, the follow-up action is not for the faint at heart. It requires leaders to step away from the hierarchical dynamic that tends to produce pride and defensiveness when being confronted. Keep in mind that different types of wounds call for different methods of treatment. A skinned knee may just need peroxide and a band-aid, but cutting a finger while cooking dinner may need a trip to the emergency room and stitches. The severity of the work wound will surely dictate the treatment approach that should align with the policies of the company. Nonetheless, if a work wound is handled respectfully and empathetically by a leader, it will establish that this exchange is not a unilateral approach but a collaborative model for conflict resolution within the company culture. For example, when a leader takes responsibility for their role in a wound, they may need to apologize.

An apology, whether public or private, can sound like this:

> "Hey Amber, yesterday in the staff meeting I said [insert offensive comment here]. After

reflection and research, I recognized how offensive that comment was. I apologize and I take full responsibility for any negative impact my words may have caused you. I am dedicated to being more intentional about the way I communicate moving forward. Is there anything you need from me or anything you'd like to say regarding the matter?"

This response to a wound ensures the person who inflicted the wound:

- Acknowledges their role in inflicting the wound.
- Avoids discounting the damage of the wound by excusing them with intentions.
- Makes a declaration of future corrected actions.
- Provides the wounded with an opportunity to restore balance through open dialogue.

If you are a leader who read this section and immediately felt excited about this pathway to open communication, I commend your commitment to actionable steps in workplace inclusivity. I imagine that many leaders who adopt this method may initially struggle with the humanistic emotions that surface from feeling exposed or confronted but will ultimately recognize the value of efficiently and genuinely addressing work wounds that could undermine team morale and success. The minimal effect of this radical approach will be perspective and insight into behaviors that contribute to negative emotional well-being while cultivating a safe and empowering process for employees to acknowledge their experiences.

Impact of Modeling

One crucial element of this work is addressing "work wounds"—everyday microaggressions or exclusionary actions that, left unchecked, can lead to stress, anxiety, or a diminished sense of occupational value for minority employees. Addressing "work wounds" as they happen is transformative because it shows that exclusionary behavior is unacceptable while fostering an environment that encourages healthy conflict, understanding, and inclusion. This kind of real-time intervention has a direct impact on mental health, as it reinforces to minority employees that they are valued and protected.

For example, if Manager A hears Manager B say to a minority team member, "Your presentation was amazing; you spoke so well," they can address the comment by pointing out that this statement implies a lower standard of communication ability based on race or ethnicity. By doing so, Manager A model's inclusivity and sets a precedent that exclusionary comments, however unintentional, are taken seriously. This transformational approach reinforces company values and supports mental health by exemplifying healthy conflict resolution in the workplace.

The implications of leadership behavior are powerful, often in unseen ways. When I came home from college one weekend, I noticed my younger sister—a sophomore in high school—had started a sneaker collection, centering on high-top Dunks, just as I had done. I asked her why she loved them so much, and with a look of disbelief, she replied, "Because you used to wear them all the time." This moment reminded me that others, especially those looking to us for guidance, watch our actions closely. As leaders, we may not always realize who is observing, but we can be sure that our behavior influences our teams. Leadership isn't about if you'll influence, but how you'll influence.

A leader who notices a microaggression can demonstrate these principles by drawing attention to the issue respectfully, showing the correct response, encourage others to remember this approach, and inspire team members to replicate it. Such interventions send a clear message of support, which can profoundly influence minority employees' mental health by reinforcing their sense of belonging and security.

Training with Intention

At the 2022 SHRM conference, I gained invaluable insights into reshaping company culture, employer policies, and HR documentation. However, an annual conference alone is not enough to support a shift to transformational leadership, especially in challenging situations. A key takeaway was HR's essential role in championing continuous training for themselves, their team, and especially the leaders of their teams. HR wields substantial power—not just in hiring and compliance but in fostering workplaces where all employees, particularly those from marginalized backgrounds, feel valued and psychologically safe. As the saying goes, "with great power comes great responsibility." HR must foster cultures where well-being is central. Inclusive practices and mental health initiatives aren't simply best practices; they're essential for creating environments where all employees feel secure and supported.

To achieve this, we as HR professionals should ensure that leaders and their teams receive consistent training in key areas such as unconscious bias, generational and cultural diversity, and psychological safety. This training builds the foundation for empathetic, non-judgmental workplaces that actively mitigate the psychological strain often faced by underrepresented employees. By empowering leaders with skills in implicit bias awareness, bystander intervention, empathy-building, and the cultivation of psychological safety, HR can support leaders in addressing workplace challenges sensitively and effectively.

When equipped with this training, leaders are better prepared to create positive interventions that shape a mentally healthy, inclusive culture. As a result, they contribute directly to the well-being of their teams and positively impact the organization's climate. In serving as the Director of HR, I've recognized my commitment to promoting ongoing training to leaders is essential not just for compliance or growth but as a transformative force that fosters a workplace where everyone feels safe, supported, and ready to thrive.

Protective Policies

Settling into my role as a human resource professional, I realized how imperative it is to seek knowledge and guidance in policy implementation and policy development. Communication with my employees revealed that the reputation of HR is not to protect the employees but to solely protect the company. In many instances, that has stood as true, however, every chance I get, I attempt to shift that narrative by how I choose to navigate the position and policies. You can decide to be in the human resource field and use your power to protect and educate the employees. These actions and upholding the expectations of the company's values do not have to be mutually exclusive. If you are up for the challenge, your insights, actions, and interference can be the catalyst to usher in congruence between the needs of your minority employees and the company's commitment to fostering a harmonious work environment that positively influences the mental health of people of color.

The American Psychological Association reported that "more than three-quarters (76%) of those who reported a toxic workplace also reported that their work environment harms their mental health, compared with fewer than one-third (28%) of those who did not report a toxic workplace" (2023).[14]

---

[14] American Psychological Association. (2023). *2023 work in America survey.* Apa.org; American Psychological Association. https://www.apa.org/pubs/reports/work-in-america/2023-workplace-health-well-being.

Diversity and mental health policies improve employee well-being, increase productivity, and reduce turnover, which are driving forces behind supporting minority employee mental health through equity (2022).[15] Diversity is merely optics until there are actions that foster inclusion and equitable practices that sustain it. Policy is the throughline to equitable practices that support inclusion, promote a sense of well-being for minority employees, and decrease negative stigma around mental health in the workplace. Inclusive and protective policies can positively affect the mental health and well-being of minority employees.

If you are HR at a company, take a moment to reflect on whether protective policies that provide access to mental health resources, such as Employee Assistance Programs (EAPs), mental health days, and flexible work arrangements, are easily accessible to minority employees. An article published by the National Association of Insurance Commissioners shed light on the statistics that in 2015, 2.1%-8% of employees were utilizing the

---

[15] U.S. Department of Health and Human Services. (2022). *Workplace Mental Health & Well-Being — Current Priorities of the U.S. Surgeon General*. Www.hhs.gov. https://www.hhs.gov/surgeongeneral/priorities/workplace-well-being/index.html.

Employee Assistance Program services organizations provide (2020).[16] This shows that even if there are EAPs available, there are only a small number of individuals who are accessing them. Think of the many barriers that are removed if companies create positive policies that resemble the following:

Example 1

Every team member is **required** to take 1 mental health day every 6 months. This day will be a paid day.

From my experience, the amount of PTO given to employees is utilized for emergencies or circumstances that may be contributing to the employee's stress. It is not ideal for an employee to have to use a PTO day for a mental health day as well. This policy will send the message that the company is prepared to give their employees additional time off not synonymous with their allotted

---

[16] Cole, C., Mccullough, K., Brooks, D., & Ling, J. (2020). *Journal of Insurance Regulation "Are We Doing Enough": An Evaluation of the Utilization of Employee Assistance Programs to Support the Mental Health Needs of Employees During the COVID-19 Pandemic. 39*(8). https://content.naic.org/sites/default/files/inline-files/JIR-ZA-39-08-EL.pdf.

PTO and employees will not be penalized for needing to take time to restore their mental capacity. This policy aligns with laws requiring mental health days for employees but bolsters these efforts by ensuring 2 paid mental health days per year separate from PTO or sick time. This affirms that the company wants its employees to work at their highest quality of self and is willing to create space and time for their employees to restore.

Example 2

Every team member is **required** to take 45 minutes of their workday to utilize the company EAP program twice every quarter.

The aspect of this policy I'd like to highlight is the ability for an employee to utilize work time to get on a call with a counselor. Most employees are superheroes in their own stories. They are hitting targets at work, caretakers for children, spouses, and parents, on committees, coaching sports, and so much more. Time is a barrier that presents itself again and again for multifaceted employees. This option, while unconventional, combats research that reveals that stress can "reduce neural firing and impair cognitive abilities" (Arnsten, 2015).[17] Imagine, if your employee experiences a "work wound", and instead of being in a space of unproductivity for the following hour they could immediately take 45 minutes to talk the situation out with a culturally competent counselor and return to their workday feeling heard, validated, and empowered. How might this embolden your team members to move from a space of clouded frustration into direction and levity? Not to mention this time, handling a work event would not take from their personal time of being a daily superhero.

I recognize that these policies are not commonly found in most companies but the adoption of these policies or policies that resemble these in your company can be the beginning of a shift to make the uncommon common. Furthermore, these policies create the story of your company's culture. It screams that as a company the employees are regarded for who they are and how they must

---

[17] Arnsten AF (2015). *Stress weakens prefrontal networks: molecular insults to higher cognition. Nat Neurosci.* (10):1376-85. doi: 10.1038/nn.4087. Epub 2015 Sep 25. PMID: 26404712; PMCID: PMC4816215.

navigate the world. Additionally, having policies that require employees to engage with behavioral health services removes the ownership of stigma that may be assigned to an individual who initiates these supports independently. These policies set a precedent signaling that the company is aware of stressors that regularly impact minority employees in and out of the workplace.

Protective Programs

In the Fall of 2023, I was working as HR Director at a therapeutic day school and noticed a sharp rise in team members struggling with mental health. My role as Director of People Equity and Culture, along with my background as a licensed clinical social worker, brought many employees to my office after hours, sharing personal and heavy life experiences. Simultaneously I was working as a mental health consultant for the company I founded, The Place of Impact, which was primarily focused on mental health coaching and training for educators and leaders. Recognizing the need for deeper support, I shifted my services, and I proposed an employee mental health group to the executive director of the organization. She excitedly accepted this partnership. This group gathered 12 employees over six weeks to explore common mental health challenges and practice coping skills. By the end, employees gained valuable tools to manage both personal and professional stress, with many sharing their positive experiences using these techniques.

This employee mental health group was funded by the organization, entirely free to participants, and held onsite immediately after work, removing barriers to travel and keeping the time commitment manageable. If you are thinking of adopting a program similar and want to encourage participation, I recommend companies offer one on-the-clock hour per week to host such sessions. If in-house facilities aren't available, organizations like *The Place of Impact* can step in to lead these valuable groups. After four cohorts I was able to serve 48 team members within the organization. The same team members who sat in my office with tears flowing were now dropping in to say, "Ms. T, I used the breathing technique we learned in group yesterday when another team member made me upset." Or "I am so proud of myself for taking the high road in this conflict I experienced over the weekend with my family member."

In addition to mental health groups, Employee Resource Groups (ERGs) offer minority employees a safe space to connect and address workplace challenges. These groups provide a platform to highlight support gaps and foster camaraderie. While ERGs are challenging to establish, they can play a significant role in building a more inclusive company culture. Companies committed to genuine support should incentivize ERGs, recognizing their value in shaping a supportive environment.

Supporting ERG leaders with stipends for organizing initiatives promotes employee engagement and demonstrates the company's commitment to inclusivity. These groups allow minority employees to address issues impacting their mental health and suggest potential solutions. Whether through an ERG or a mental health group, it's essential to provide spaces where minority employees can share experiences and learn coping strategies, ultimately enhancing their well-being and contribution to a positive workplace.

Conclusion

Creating an inclusive, supportive workplace relies on leaders' ongoing commitment and advocacy. Supporting minority employees' well-being involves diversifying hiring, developing protective policies, and fostering inclusivity in daily actions and conversations. Be a leader or organization that prioritizes diversity, mental health, and policies that promote employee well-being.

Remember, the standard doesn't shift if you don't.

SHIFT Framework

Being in leadership for almost a decade and my experience as the Director of HR gave me insight on the need for a shift in workplace culture and practices to better support minority mental health. The SHIFT framework provides a comprehensive approach to addressing minority mental health in the workplace. It encourages proactive steps towards positive change.

Support Mental Health Initiatives

Focuses on actively promoting and facilitating mental health support in the workplace. This element encourages organizations to take concrete steps to support the well-being of minority employees.

Heal Work Wounds

Emphasizes the importance of creating processes for reflection, accountability, and restoration processes when these incidents occur. It involves recognizing, addressing, and healing the psychological impacts of microaggressions, discrimination, and other negative experiences that minority employees face in the workplace. This component encourages leaders to lead by example, promoting inclusivity and mental health awareness.

Implement Protective Policies, Practices & Programs

Stresses the importance of developing and enforcing policies that safeguard minority employees' mental health and promote equity.

Foster Supportive Spaces

Highlights the necessity of creating safe and nurturing environments for minority employees. These spaces allow employees to share experiences, find support, and build community, contributing to collective healing and empowerment.

Train for Cultural Competence

Reveals the importance of comprehensive training programs that enhance cultural competence, awareness of implicit biases, and understanding of mental health issues. This element highlights the crucial role of leadership in creating an inclusive and supportive workplace culture.

Tateanna Foster, LCSW

Tateanna Foster is an experienced mental health leader with almost a decade of expertise in empowering individuals and organizations through her work in social work and mental health consulting. She earned her master's degree in social work from the University of Illinois, Urbana-Champaign, with a minor in Leadership Studies in 2016, and has since been dedicated to serving diverse communities and transforming workplace cultures.

Tateanna began her career in 2017 as the lead social worker at a therapeutic day school, where she supported diverse learners and their families. In 2019, she developed and led an early childhood program until 2021, laying the groundwork for early interventions and development support. Currently, she serves as the Director of People, Equity, and Culture, where her leadership focuses on fostering inclusive environments that promote equity and well-being for all.

As a sought-after presenter, Tateanna has shared her knowledge with numerous audiences, delivering impactful sessions at conferences, district trainings, and community organizations. Notable presentations/partnerships include the 2024 Michigan Counseling Association Conference, an international presentation at the Pan African Congress on Autism in Nairobi, Kenya, and an ongoing partnership with the Angels Athletics Youth Development Program. Her unique background has equipped her with expertise in supporting mental health initiatives for youth, parents, educators, professionals, and organizational leaders.

Tateanna is also the Founder and Impact Leader of The Place of Impact, a mental health consulting company aimed at empowering individuals and organizations to navigate life's mental health challenges. She partners with communities to host mental health festivals featuring yoga, breathwork, art therapy, and resources. Additionally, she has provided employee mental health support groups for employees in the educational sector. Tateanna is passionate about using psychoeducation to equip individuals with tools to lead boldly and effectively in cross-cultural and complex environments.

5 | Fatimah Turner, PhD

Concrete Dreams: Pink Crowns and Golden Pedestals

The walls of the public housing complex stood tall around me, not just as boundaries, but as silent witnesses to the strength and resilience that would define my journey. Raised in a maze of identical buildings with only color-coded doors as distinguishing features, my dreams and determination knew no bounds. My parents, barely out of their teens, grappled with poverty and addiction. Their struggles cast shadows of stigma over my childhood, yet it was within these very shadows that I learned to find my own light.

Determined to change the trajectory of my life, I purposely ventured out, desperately trying to escape and break free from the harsh realities that had defined my family and community. This deliberate quest for a different future led me down a path I could scarcely have imagined. The girl from the orange-colored door would one day wear a different kind of identifier—a pink crown of expectations standing on a golden pedestal of representation. This crown, heavy with the hopes and dreams of my village, and this pedestal, elevating me to a position of visibility while paradoxically rendering me invisible, would become central to my experience as a highly educated Black woman. This is the story of my journey from concrete dreams to the weight of a pink crown and the precarious balance of a golden pedestal, and how I learned to navigate the complex realities they represent.

My childhood was far from a fairytale. In addition to public housing, I endured physical and sexual abuse, witnessed drug transactions and violence in my own home, lived in and out of battered women's shelters, and often spent my nights lying awake, protecting my little brother from whatever dangers might find their way to our Orange Door. The challenges of my early years became the forge that tempered my spirit. My parents' battles with adversity, while painful to witness, taught me invaluable lessons about perseverance and the power of a dream.

I have always been a dreamer, a fairytale princess in my head of sorts. My father told me I was the daughter of a king, and I believed him with all my heart. It was my defense mechanism, how I mentally set myself apart from the harsh realities around me. These dreams, rather than my parents' struggles, became the fuel for my ambitions. Life taught me early on that no hero would save me—I would need to be the heroine in my own story.

This challenging and often traumatic upbringing, against all odds, became my secret weapon. My experiences honed my ability to adapt, to find creative solutions with limited resources, and to see opportunities where others might be blinded by obstacles. The survival skills I cultivated in those early years—the sharp awareness of my surroundings, the ability to code-switch, the art of finesse, and the determination to push through seemingly insurmountable barriers—these would become the very roots that nourished my growth in worlds far removed from the orange doors where my dreams were seeded.

The intersection of my race, gender, and socio-economic status marked me with a stigma that felt like a crushing weight. My family's involvement with drugs was no secret in our community, and the shadow of addiction loomed large over our lives. Weekends often found me in the sterile visiting rooms of maximum security prisons, while at home, I watched my mother cycle through a series of abusive relationships. From a young age, I became acutely aware of how the world perceived me differently.

This harsh reality hit home when my best friend's mother refused to let her stay at my house, citing concerns about exposing her daughter to situations that conflicted with their moral values. In that moment, I realized I was carrying the burden of my parents' choices and circumstances—a weight I neither asked for nor deserved, yet one that would shape my path forward.

What seemed like a singular incident at the time cast a long shadow over my life, its impact reverberating through my childhood and well into adulthood. This seemingly insignificant event weighed heavily on my mind and heart, shaping my self-perception and influencing my behavior in ways I couldn't fully comprehend at the time. As I grew older and became a parent myself, I found these internalized judgments had seeped into the very framework of my parenting style. In an attempt to distance myself and my children from the stigma I had experienced, I became hyper-focused on holding myself and my daughters to an unrealistic moral standard. This manifested in a parenting approach that, while well-intentioned, bordered on emotionally abusive at times. The weight of that long-ago rejection had transformed into a generational burden, one I was unknowingly passing on in my desperate attempt to prove our worth to a world that had once deemed us unworthy.

The weight of this stigma was, and at times still can be, debilitating. It's almost like carrying around someone else's dirty, smelly laundry and watching others avoid you and say you smell. Even though the laundry or smell isn't yours, it still affects you. People still judge you by it. Even when others don't judge you by it, you still judge yourself by it. In my ongoing efforts to distance myself from this perceived taint, I tried to speak extra proper, to be extra virtuous, and to be extra smart, careful to limit my male interactions lest the world see me as "loose." Ultimately, I was trying to gain the world's trust, desperately attempting to be seen as something other than the daughter of a dope fiend.

Yet, amidst this struggle, I found beacons of hope and guidance. The nurturing and convincing words of my grandmothers provided a crucial counterbalance to this stigma. They both walked with a dignity that I yearned to emulate, a quiet strength that I tried to absorb through osmosis. They reminded me, with unwavering conviction, that I could achieve anything I set my mind to. My sheros held me to a standard of self-respect that became my north star.

I keenly observed the women around me, like my teachers Ms. Ross and Ms. Pollock, studying their mannerisms, their speech, their very essence. I leaned into Ms. Hernandez's love for arts and culture. I took what I could from the people in my circle of service, piecing together a new image of myself, brick by brick. All the while, my Nana's words echoed in my ears: "Don't tell them, show them" became more than just a guiding light—they became my battle cry. Fueled by the strength of my grandmothers and the examples set by the women I admired, I set out to rewrite my story.

I was the first and only one of my siblings to graduate from college, and I was the only one to avoid drugs or jail. After earning my associate's degree, I pushed on to earn my bachelor's, then two master's degrees, and finally, a Ph.D. And I did all of this as a single mom working full time, each achievement a testament to the resilience I had forged in the crucible of my youth.

As I progressed, the landscape of my life transformed dramatically. The orange-colored doors of my public housing complex eventually faded into the manicured lawns of college campuses where I was both student and instructor. The brick city towers of my childhood gave way to ivory towers where ideas and intellect became my new currency. It was a metamorphosis both exhilarating and disorienting, a journey that would bring its own unique challenges and revelations.

Just as I began to acclimate to this new world, the weight of a crown of expectation settled heavily on my shoulders. I carried the hopes of every cousin who never made it out, every aunt working multiple jobs, every neighbor who looked at me with hope, and every Black woman who had walked in my heels, flats, and slippers. This weight represented my parents, who did their best with what they had; my grandmother, who believed I could do anything; my ancestors, who could only dream of such opportunities; and my sister, a victim of her surroundings, who died at 29. Most importantly, I carried it for my daughters, vowing they would never bear this 300-pound bag of someone else's dirty laundry.

Juggling these collective hopes, fears, and aspirations overwhelmed me in ways I wasn't prepared for. Yet, I understood my unspoken assignment: to succeed for the sake of us all.

Imposter Invasion: Battling the Voices of Doubt

The pressure to succeed was relentless, accompanied by the sage words of the elders warning that "Failure is not an option." It was a burden I bore silently because that's what strong Black women do. We endure. We persevere. We make it look easy. But oh, how heavy that crown became. Adorned with the dreams of generations and studded with the sacrifices of those who came before me, I wore it proudly. Inside, however, I was crumbling. The fear of letting it slip, of being seen as lazy or a failure, was paralyzing. To show weakness was unthinkable. To ask for help? Unbecoming...

As I climbed higher, the weight of the crown only intensified. Each accomplishment brought with it a new chorus of voices, both encouraging and discouraging. I heard TLC's warning to stop chasing waterfalls echo in my mind as I walked into lecture halls and boardrooms. "Just stick to the rivers and lakes that you're used to," it seemed to hiss as I reached for opportunities far beyond my childhood circumstances. These conflicting messages had me questioning my every move, side-eyeing my own achievements even as I accepted awards and accolades.

The pressure became so overwhelming that I found myself reassessing whether I truly deserved to escape the poverty-stricken environment of my birth. The crown of expectations grew heavier, and the pedestal of representation felt increasingly precarious. It was in this state of internal turmoil that I first encountered two concepts that would name my struggle: imposter syndrome and achievement guilt. These twin phenomena—the feeling of being a fraud despite my accomplishments and the guilt of succeeding where many of my loved ones had not—created a perfect storm of self-doubt and emotional conflict.

Imposter syndrome whispered that I didn't belong, that my achievements were flukes. On the other hand, achievement guilt made me question whether I deserved success, especially when so many others in my community were still struggling. As a Black woman who grew up in poverty, this internal conflict was especially intense. Often, our upbringing instills a collectivist mindset, emphasizing the importance of caring for our families and communities for our survival and perceived success. The question, "Am I my brother's keeper?" wasn't just a platitude but a deeply ingrained responsibility.

Adding to this complexity were the implicit and explicit conflicting messages from family and community. On one hand, I heard, "We need your help. You're our hope." On the other, there were whispers of, "You think you're better; "she's all bougie now." These contradictory sentiments tugged at me from opposite directions, making the crown heavier and the pedestal more unstable. The term "bougie" (derived from bourgeois) carried with it accusations of forgetting my roots, of adopting airs and graces that separated me from my community.

It was a cutting reminder of the delicate balance I had to maintain between progress and loyalty to my hood.

For Black women, especially those from disadvantaged backgrounds, these feelings can be particularly intense. People rarely view our success as an individual achievement, but rather as a reflection of our entire community. This adds layers of complexity to our journey. We're expected to climb the ladder of success, but also to reach back and pull others up with us. The weight of this responsibility, combined with the lingering doubts about our worthiness, can create a unique and challenging psychological burden.

As I grappled with these conflicting emotions, I realized that my experience was not unique. Many of us who have "made it out" find ourselves straddling two worlds, never quite fitting in either. We carry the hopes and dreams of our communities on our shoulders, even as we question our right to occupy the spaces we've worked so hard to enter. This tension between individual achievement and collective responsibility, between wearing the crown proudly and maintaining balance on the pedestal, would become a recurring theme in my journey, shaping both my personal growth and my professional path.

As I grappled with these internal conflicts and external pressures, I found myself facing yet another paradox in my professional journey. The higher I climbed, the more I became aware of a phenomenon that seemed unique to Black women in spaces of power and influence—a state of being both hypervisible and unseen.

Hypervisible Yet Unseen

As I navigated my career, I found myself grappling with this paradoxical experience shared by many Black women in professional spaces—the phenomenon of simultaneous hypervisibility and invisibility. As I climbed the ladder of success, this duality became increasingly apparent, placing me on an ever-higher pedestal.

The pedestal, while seemingly a place of honor, became a precarious and isolating position. It was both visible and invisible, tangible and intangible. On one hand, I was hypervisible—my presence as a Black woman in spaces traditionally dominated by others made me stand out, often positioning me as the 'representative' of my race and gender. Both allies and adversaries scrutinized every action, every word, and every decision I made.

This elevated position brought both opportunity and obligation. It represented the expectations placed upon me by my family, community, and society—some explicitly stated, others merely perceived or assumed by me. Built from the hopes of those who came before me and the aspirations of those who looked to me as an example, the pedestal became a symbol of success for others to strive towards. Yet, it also left me straddling two worlds—no longer fully part of the community in which I grew up and not quite fitting into my new professional sphere. An outsider within.

Upon entering professional settings with a light brown curly afro, hoop earrings, and skin that was copper-tanned to conventional perfection, I did receive instant and rapt physical attention. At the same time, I was frequently overlooked and unseen when it came to doling out resources or granting opportunities. This duality multiplied as I climbed the ladder of success.

Yet, paradoxically, even as I stood elevated on this pedestal, I felt invisible. My unique perspectives, struggles, and the nuances of my experience often went unseen or unacknowledged. Stereotypes and preconceptions frequently overshadowed my individuality. People seemed to focus on the color of my skin, my gender, and my background story, but they overlooked the real me—the person behind the labels, the individual striving to earn and deserve everything I possessed.

In meetings, I could feel all eyes on me, waiting for me to speak. Was I truly expected to be the voice of all Black women, or was this an assumption I'd internalized? My successes were celebrated loudly, held up as examples of diversity and inclusion working well. But this visibility came with a price—the pressure, both external and self-imposed, to be perfect, to never show weakness, to always be "on."

The higher the pedestal, the more intense the spotlight became. People often introduced me as "the single mother who...", "the only Black woman in...", or, more specifically, "the girl from public housing who became..." These labels, while acknowledging my achievements, also served to separate me from my peers and heighten the sense that I was different, exceptional—a unicorn in these spaces. They put my background on display, making my journey from poverty to professional a constant part of my narrative, whether I wanted it to be or not.

This invisibility manifested in various ways. In brainstorming sessions, I'd offer an idea only to have it ignored, only to hear it praised when repeated by a white colleague minutes later. Blank stares or awkward silences often met my cultural references and experiences, reminding me of the gap between my world and theirs. All eyes would turn to me when discussions of diversity arose, expecting me to educate and explain, but when I spoke about my lived experiences, they often dismissed me as being "too sensitive" or "making everything about race."

The exhaustion of this constant toggle between hypervisibility and invisibility, between meeting perceived expectations and asserting my true self, was real. It meant code-switching not just in how I spoke, but in how I presented myself, how I expressed my emotions, how I wore my hair, and how I navigated professional spaces. It meant carrying the weight of representation while also fighting to be seen as an individual.

The persistence of the survival mode, even after achieving success, added to these complex dynamics. The hypervigilance that kept me alive in difficult environments persisted in boardrooms and academic spaces. This survival mode, honed at the crucible of poverty and adversity, became both a strength and a burden in my new environment. I found myself hoarding opportunities out of a deep-seated fear that they might suddenly disappear.

Every project, every networking event, every chance to prove myself—it became something I couldn't pass up, even if it meant working myself to exhaustion. My family didn't only depend on me to be successful for image purposes; I was responsible for the well-being of my children and my sister's and brother's children. I was, and am, indeed my brother's keeper. This added responsibility amplified the pressure to succeed and maintain my hard-won position, as so many lives depended on my continued success.

Trust, or rather the lack of it, became another hallmark of this persistent survival mode. Having learned early on that reliance on others could lead to disappointment or danger, I struggled to fully trust colleagues or mentors. This made delegation difficult and collaboration challenging. I often found myself taking on more than I could handle, convinced that it was safer to do everything myself than to risk depending on others.

From this confluence of experiences—imposter syndrome, achievement guilt, hypervisibility, invisibility, and persistent survival mode—emerged what we now call "Black Girl Magic." This phrase, born out of necessity and resilience, became both a celebration and armor for Black women like me navigating spaces not designed for our success. "Black Girl Magic" became our way of reclaiming our narrative. It was a response to a world that often failed to recognize our brilliance, our hard work, or our multifaceted nature.

Be not mistaken; this "Magic" came at a cost. The expectation of always being magical—to make the impossible look easy—added another layer of pressure to our already heavy load. At times, it seemed as though we needed to surpass human capabilities to gain respect. Despite its intended empowerment, the phrase could also act as a barrier, establishing an unattainable benchmark of unwavering strength and success. Moreover, this perception of magical ability often led others to believe we didn't need support or assistance. It seemed as though we possessed a mysterious enchantment that enabled us to effortlessly surmount any challenge. This misconception further isolated us, making it even harder to ask for help or show any sign of vulnerability. The "magic" that was supposed to celebrate our resilience often became the very thing that denied us the right to be human, to struggle, to need support just like anyone else.

In the balance, there was undeniable power in this concept. It created a sisterhood, a shared understanding among Black women facing similar challenges, especially women who came from where I came from. While as Black women we share similar experiences, we also do not share the exact same experiences or perspectives, depending on our cultural and socioeconomic backgrounds. This nuance is crucial to recognize. Still, "Black Girl Magic" gave us language to celebrate each other's achievements in a world that often overlooked them. It became a source of pride—a way to honor the generations of Black women who had paved the way for us, particularly those who had overcome similar obstacles of poverty and stigma.

Rewriting the Rules of Success

The very experiences that could have been our greatest obstacles have become our most powerful assets. The hypervigilance that once kept us safe in challenging environments has transformed into an acute awareness that allows us to navigate complex social and professional landscapes. Our ability to code-switch, born from necessity, has become a valuable tool for building bridges across diverse communities.

The cognitive flexibility, or "art of finesse," required to survive in resource-limited environments has equipped us with exceptional problem-solving skills and creativity in our professional lives. This mental agility, honed through years of adapting to ever-changing circumstances, allows us to approach challenges from multiple angles and find innovative solutions where others might see dead ends. The art of finesse we've mastered helps us navigate delicate situations with grace and effectiveness, turning potential conflicts into opportunities for growth and understanding.

The strength we developed in facing adversity has become the foundation for our perseverance in breaking through glass ceilings and creating spaces for ourselves where none existed before. Our ability to read and adapt to various social contexts, along with our resilience, has uniquely equipped us to lead and innovate in diverse professional environments.

As we continue to navigate the paradoxes of hypervisibility and invisibility—of the crown and the pedestal—we must remember to draw strength from our roots. The lessons learned in those color-coded buildings, the resilience forged in overcoming early adversities, the adaptability developed in bridging different worlds—these are not burdens to escape but powerful tools to wield.

In embracing our full stories—challenges and triumphs alike—we redefine what success looks like. We show that it's possible to honor where we come from while charting new territories. We show that the advantages we've gained from our disadvantages have given us unique perspectives and strengths that are crucial in decision-making environments.

As we lift each other up and create spaces for vulnerability and authentic self-expression, we're not just achieving individual success—we're reshaping the narrative for all Black women. We're proving that our magic isn't about being superhuman but about being fully, unapologetically human, with all the complexity that entails.

In the end, our crowns may be heavy and our pedestals high, but they are also testaments to the incredible journeys we've undertaken. We stand tall not in spite of where we come from, but because of it. Our experiences have not just shaped us; they've empowered us to shape the world around us. And in doing so, we're not just chasing waterfalls—we're creating new ones, carving out paths where none existed before, for ourselves and for generations to come.

That is the true essence of our magic—not just surviving, but thriving and transforming the landscape as we go. It's a magic born not of comfort, but of struggle; not of perfection, but of perseverance. And it's a magic that, having been forged in the fires of adversity, will never be dimmed.

CROWN Framework: Pink Crowns and Golden Pedestals

The Crown Framework describes the complex psychological and social dynamics experienced by individuals, particularly Black women from disadvantaged backgrounds, who achieve significant professional and academic success. The framework uses the metaphor of a "pink crown" to represent the unique burden of expectations, responsibilities, and representation that accompanies achievement.

The CROWN Framework

Carrying Collective Expectations

Carrying collective expectations means shouldering the hopes and dreams of both family and community while navigating the unique pressures of being a trailblazer. This responsibility involves carefully balancing the weight of representation in professional spaces, particularly when you find yourself as a "first" or "only" in your field. It's about understanding how to honor the legacy of those who came before you while simultaneously forging new paths forward. This element of the crown recognizes that your success isn't just personal—it's a beacon of possibility for future generations, creating pathways that others can follow.

Resilience Through Recognition

Resilience through recognition encompasses the vital practice of acknowledging both your achievements and the challenges you've overcome. It involves transforming past struggles into professional strengths while actively managing the complex emotions of imposter syndrome and achievement guilt. This aspect of the crown focuses on embracing your unique value and perspective, understanding that your lived experiences contribute meaningfully to your professional capabilities. It's about building sustainable success practices that honor both where you've come from and where you're going, creating a foundation for long-term achievement without burning out.

Owning Your Space

Owning your space requires masterful navigation to be simultaneously hypervisible and invisible in professional environments. It means developing an authentic leadership presence while strategically code-switching to effectively communicate across different contexts. This element involves confidently creating and claiming your professional territory while maintaining your authentic self. It's about setting and maintaining healthy boundaries that protect your energy and dignity, ensuring you can sustain your presence in spaces not traditionally designed for you while making them more accessible for others who will follow.

Wielding Your Wisdom

Wielding your wisdom means strategically leveraging the survival skills and intuition developed through life experience in professional contexts. It transforms hypervigilance into an asset of heightened awareness and strategic thinking. This aspect of the crown celebrates the "art of finesse"— the ability to navigate complex situations with grace and effectiveness. It's about recognizing how your adaptability can drive innovation and seeing challenges as opportunities for growth and transformation. This wisdom, born from experience, becomes a powerful tool for leadership and change.

Nurturing Networks

Nurturing networks involves intentionally building bridges between your community of origin and your professional sphere. It means creating robust support systems that span different spaces while maintaining authentic connections in both. This element of the crown emphasizes the importance of both mentoring others and continuing to seek mentorship throughout your journey. It involves strategic sharing of resources and opportunities, ensuring that as you climb, you create sturdy ladders for others. Most importantly, it's about maintaining strong connections to your roots while growing new branches that extend your influence and impact.

Remember: The CROWN framework is dynamic and interconnected. Each element requires constant attention and balance, with success defined by your ability to manage all aspects while maintaining your well-being. Adapt the framework to your unique circumstances, always remembering that strong support systems are essential for sustainable achievement. Most importantly, understand that the weight of your crown, while sometimes heavy, can become your greatest source of strength and impact.

Fatimah Turner, PhD

Fatimah Turner, Ph.D., emerged from the vibrant streets of Newark, New Jersey, where her early life shaped her understanding of community, resilience, and the power of education. A mother of three girls, she masterfully balances her roles as an academic, entrepreneur, and parent while continuing to serve the community that raised her.

As the founder and owner of Inner City Café, she has created more than just a pink-hued gathering space—she's established a sanctuary where urban culture, comfort, and community converge. This entrepreneurial venture reflects her commitment to fostering spaces that nurture both body and spirit in the heart of the city.

Dr. Turner's academic journey led her from the classrooms of Newark to earning her doctorate in Family Science & Human Development from Montclair State University, along with master's degrees in Educational Leadership and Social Work. Her research focuses on family diversity, African American extended family networks, and the experiences of first-generation college students, drawing inspiration from her own path and the stories of those around her.

As a licensed clinical social worker and educator, she brings her wealth of experience to both the classroom and the community. Her Newark roots and her dedication to uplifting urban communities continue to inform her work, whether in academia or at her café. Dr. Turner currently serves on the

Orange Board of Education, embodying her belief that education and community service are inseparable paths to social change.

Her writing explores themes of family dynamics, urban resilience, and the intricate tapestry of Black community life, informed by both her professional expertise and personal experiences as a mother, entrepreneur, and daughter of Newark.

6 | Jessica Leigh

Blue Horizon: Healing Through a Spiritual Lens

Imagine a man in his mid-forties, visibly anxious and finding it hard to maintain eye contact. He shared that he and his wife had lived separately for three years. Their romance blossomed during a mission trip, and he felt a deep calling to continue his missionary work, eventually becoming a leader at a missionary base. However, his wife did not share this passion for missionary life and opted to live and work in the city instead. He was hesitant to discuss their situation honestly with her, fearing it could lead to divorce—a prospect he believed would disqualify him from his missionary work.

Moreover, he was reluctant to disclose the state of his failing marriage, which he viewed as beyond repair, to his parents, supporting churches, and the faith community at his workplace. He worried about being perceived as a moral failure, disappointing his parents and supporters, and potentially losing financial support in the event of a divorce. These fears had deterred him from seeking counseling for years.

This account underscores the complex interplay of faith, mental health, and personal challenges many religious communities navigate. It emphasizes that faith and mental health are not separate grounds but deeply interconnected aspects of human experience. Mental health issues are just as prevalent in religious communities as they are in the broader society.[18] However, there is a significant reluctance within these communities to accept mental health care fully. This hesitation largely stems from an inability to overcome the stigma associated with mental health.

Drawing from my 17 years of experience working within faith communities, split between a church

---

[18] Hope, A. O. (2019b, September 5). *Christian Mental Health Statistics — Anthem of Hope.* Christian Mental Health, Suicide Prevention, Mental Health, Depression. Retrieved September 15, 2024, from https://anthemofhope.org/blog/2019/9/5/christian-mental-health-statistics.

setting and an international missionary organization, I have observed a consistent trend. Most of those seeking counseling were not high-level leaders but middle-level leaders, staff, and students. This observation raises questions about senior leaders' perceptions and responses to mental health issues. Despite often advocating for mental health care and encouraging others to seek counseling, their reluctance to discuss or admit their own mental health struggles suggests a stigma. This hesitancy to openly address their mental health issues sends a mixed message for fear of being perceived as emotionally unstable. It may inadvertently reinforce shame around mental health struggles despite the outward advocacy for mental health care.

In exploring the profound depths of our faith journeys, a few critical questions emerge: Why do we often hesitate to weave psychology into our spiritual narratives? What barriers keep us from acknowledging that, as psychological beings, our spirituality is inherently entwined with our mental well-being? The intersection of psychology, spirituality, and mental health care within faith communities presents a complex yet intriguing area of study. Understanding these dynamics can unlock valuable insights that enhance our faith experience and promote holistic well-being. A recent case study highlights the potential connection between mental health and spirituality, offering useful insights into this relationship.

Integrating mental health with spirituality invites us to reflect on important questions: "Do our deeply held beliefs genuinely align with the core values and practices of our faith?" or "Are these beliefs simply skewed perceptions that serve our selfish ambitions?" Our worldviews, whether conscious or unconscious, significantly influence our actions. By examining these perspectives, we can uncover insights into our fears and underlying motivations, allowing us to align our beliefs and actions more closely with the highest aspirations of our faith.

Therefore, it is essential to understand that spirituality and mental health within faith communities are not distinct disciplines but rather interconnected strands. This integration can significantly enhance and deepen the spiritual journey when approached holistically. Without such integration, faith might flounder, resulting in apathy and mindless religious practices. As mental health professionals in these settings, we care for the heart, recognizing that our actions stem from this core. Our approach must consider the whole person—spiritual, emotional, relational, and physical aspects—to truly care for and nurture holistic well-being.

This chapter delves into the vital role mental health workers can play within faith communities, underscoring the challenges and the unique opportunities to fortify faith through a holistic approach to mental health care. It also highlights the crucial interplay between mental health and spirituality in faith communities, offering insights and practical advice for mental health professionals working in these distinctive environments. The following content outlines a structured approach to managing the complexities found at this intersection, aiming to guide professionals in navigating these challenges effectively.

Navigating Faith in Mental Health Practice

Serving as a mental health professional in a faith community is more than a career—it is a calling that demands a deep commitment to holistic well-being. This vocation requires practitioners to positively impact lives while navigating personal growth and challenges. The spiritual dimension of this work infuses it with profound meaning, uplifting it beyond the boundaries of a typical profession.

The interconnection between mental health and spirituality in faith communities is intricate and profound. Mental health workers in these settings must consider a holistic approach to wellbeing, encompassing emotional health, mental clarity, physical well-being, relational connections, spiritual growth and fulfillment, and a sense of purpose. Neglecting any of these aspects can diminish effectiveness and lead to burnout.

In the heart of faith communities, humility is an essential virtue. Mental health professionals in these settings offer more than just their therapeutic expertise; they bring their whole selves, complete with personal experiences and stories, to those who confide in them. These caregivers integrate their faith, calling, and deep passion for nurturing others into their practice. This selfless commitment is noble and rewarding, as it allows them to witness individuals gain the confidence to navigate their life's journey.

However, the journey has its challenges. There are moments when the stories shared by clients are so overwhelming that the only response is to offer silent, empathetic companionship, sharing in their sorrow. These experiences remind us that we, too, carry our own burdens and that our stories intertwine with those we aim to support. In these interactions, the boundaries between "I-and-you" fade, fostering a "we" built on genuine connection and mutual growth. This dynamic relationship opens the door for learning, as our clients' experiences offer us invaluable insights.

As faith-based mental health professionals, our role is not to position ourselves as experts but rather as fellow sojourners on a shared human journey, deeply engaging with each individual's unique story. This perspective enables us to grow and evolve alongside those we serve, enhancing our capacity to provide meaningful care within our communities. In doing so, we support others and deepen our understanding and compassion, embracing humanity.

Embracing humility allows us to acknowledge our limitations and accept that we are imperfect, prone to mistakes, and do not have all the answers. This humble stance fosters an environment of non-judgment and openness, where those in our care can experience a sense of safety, belonging, and love. Crucially, it encourages us to accept ourselves fully—helping us to avoid projecting our insecurities onto others. Thus, self-acceptance is central to our spiritual journey and a fundamental expression of humility.

The challenges faced by mental health professionals in faith communities stretch beyond personal struggles. There is often an unspoken expectation that these individuals should have answers to life's essential questions, embody unwavering strength, and exemplify moral perfection. This pressure is not limited to them but applies to anyone with spiritual respect and authority. Over time, these unrealistic expectations can cause a rift between their public image and authentic self. Guided by perceived expectations, it can lead to burnout and, potentially, immorality or ethical lapses.

Mental health professionals within faith communities have a unique opportunity to positively influence their congregation by incorporating spirituality into their practice. They navigate the delicate balance between meeting high expectations and embracing the commonality of human experiences, finding genuine connections in moments of failure, and discovering strength during times of despair. These professionals are honored to provide support and guidance, sharing a part of individuals' journeys and safeguarding their emotional well-being.

One counselor noted how this approach transformed her practice. When clients came to her feeling lost, abandoned, or questioning their faith due to persistent hardships, she drew on her own experiences of wrestling with unanswered prayers. She helped them understand that spiritual growth often occurs because of challenges.

Integrating mental health and spirituality allows practitioners to foster a healing environment that respects the entirety of an individual– encompassing the body, mind, and spirit. This holistic approach recognizes and celebrates each person's inherent dignity and value. It paves the way for a journey filled with hope, resilience, and transformative growth for professionals and their clients.

Integrative Care: Blending Spiritual and Mental Health Practices

It is not uncommon to revisit familiar challenges, a reality that applies universally and extends to those within the mental health profession. This shared experience serves as a poignant reminder of our human frailty and the inherent limitations of our knowledge. The journey of life, with its myriad challenges and setbacks, both humbles us and underscores our insignificance within the broader expanse of the cosmos.

Therefore, we are encouraged to embrace the myriad challenges that life presents, viewing each as an opportunity for personal growth and enlightenment. In doing so, we foster a sense of solidarity and mutual support, illuminating the path for ourselves and others. This collective journey towards understanding and empathy enriches our individual lives and contributes to a more compassionate and connected world. Therefore, we leverage our shared struggles to inspire us toward a more meaningful and purposeful life.

Clients generally know that spirituality is part of integrated care if we work within a faith community. In cases where clients do not share the same religious beliefs, they will be informed about the mental health professionals' religious orientation and approach to providing spiritually integrated care to respect the spiritual aspect of the clients' lives. Working in a faith-based organization may lead to relational boundaries and roles overlapping. It is essential to clearly define our role as mental health professionals to clients, ensuring a safe space for them to feel comfortable exploring the intersection of their mental health and struggles of faith. Whether or not we work in a faith-based setting, including a general mental health professional code of conduct and ethics is always a good practice.

While following suggested spiritual care practices may seem like a lengthy list, incorporating these practices into your life can ensure a balanced approach to serving in your faith community, always guided by a heart full of genuine love and care. Consider adopting the following practices for spiritual self-care:

Craft a Personal Mission Statement

Having a mission statement will bring us back to the initial reasons for starting our journey in mental health care. The mission statement should reflect our deepest desires for what we aim to accomplish through our work. The following statement is an AI-generated example:

My mission is to "empower individuals to achieve holistic well-being by providing compassionate, client-centered mental health counseling that honors their unique spiritual beliefs, fostering a space for meaningful exploration and personal growth through the integration of psychological and spiritual insights and practices."

Know Your Religious Beliefs

A deep understanding of your religious beliefs is vital. Mental clarity is closely linked to a thorough understanding of our beliefs. This process involves actively engaging with challenging questions and mysteries that may cause discomfort rather than avoiding them. Even though it might be difficult, deeply examining our beliefs is crucial to spiritual growth. It tests and strengthens our faith, providing a solid foundation to help us navigate the ups and downs of our spiritual journey.

Cultivate a Prayer Life

Prayer is essential to maintaining spiritual health. It makes God more tangible and personal, moving us away from the illusion of control and self-sufficiency. It is not just about asking for what we need and desire; it is an opportunity to connect with the divine and truly listen to the voice of God. Prayer is a dialogue, not merely a time of listing desires and expecting God to fulfill them.

Practice the Presence of God

Engaging in the practice of God's presence is another form of prayer—wordless prayer. It involves sitting in silence, with the understanding that God exists and is interacting with our spirit. This practice begins with a deep breathing exercise, which helps us center ourselves. From there, we transition into mindfulness, immersing ourselves fully in the present moment while connecting with our body, mind, and emotions. Next, we focus on staying in the presence of God within us, allowing our thoughts to drift while gently returning our awareness to that divine presence.

Keep a Gratitude Journal

Gratitude helps us transition from a physical to a spiritual perspective, teaching us to find appreciation amidst life's trials and pains. It may seem unnatural at first, as our default reaction often leans toward complaint and distress. However, holding onto the belief that gratitude is reserved for moments when life is going well means missing out on its true essence. Starting our journal entries with the challenges we face, acknowledging them, and finding reasons to be grateful can be transformative.

Practice Letting Go

"Let go and let God" is frequently expressed in a hopeless situation. We may be underestimating the profundity of the nature of letting go or surrendering control. For many, this is a daunting task. It often requires addressing mental health issues tied to the need for control. Even more challenging is not just the willingness to surrender control of a desire but also releasing the lingering yearning for it, which can subtly undermine our efforts to let go entirely. A closer look at our struggle with control reveals that fear is an underlying factor—the fear of not achieving our desired outcomes or being seen as a failure. This fear can leave us stuck, causing indecision or inaction on our spiritual journeys. We might justify our hesitation by saying we are praying for clear signs.

However, the previous mindset misapprehends the role of God, treating Him more like an insurance policy for our ambitions than a sovereign being. True surrender involves embracing life's uncertainty and recognizing that the only sure thing is the choices we make each day. It encourages us to be open to unexpected outcomes, trusting in God's goodness and supreme authority beyond our comprehension. Surrendering is an act of complete trust in God, finding rest in the knowledge that, no matter what happens, we are in capable hands. This surrender liberates us from constantly needing to choose "correctly." It is likened to a child deeply engrossed in play, fully confident that their parents oversee and will provide direction if necessary. Surrender is a lifelong commitment to releasing control, requiring us to be patient with ourselves and to trust in divine timing.

Schedule a Retreat in Solitude

Retreats in solitude can be practiced anywhere, but separating yourself from your usual surroundings can significantly change your mind, allowing for physical, emotional, and spiritual rejuvenation. Nature offers an ideal setting where distractions and interruptions are minimized. By removing these distractions, we can better attend to the impact of media, daily responsibilities, and the anxieties and fears that typically dominate our lives. Solitude retreats offer a dedicated space and time for deep reflection and processing, enabling us to gain valuable insights.

Such retreats are crucial for refreshing ourselves and reconnecting with our core identity, our calling, and the essence of our spirituality. Taking time for solitude is an act of self-love, fundamentally different from selfishness. Selfishness focuses solely on oneself, whereas self-love is about embracing and internalizing divine love, leading to self-forgetfulness. We must regularly rest and replenish ourselves with this divine essence to keep our inner resources. Retreats in solitude thus open the path for continuous replenishment of our physical and spiritual being, empowering us to serve our faith communities from a higher self.

Get Involved with a Faith Community

Faith communities provide a unique space for belonging and unity by engaging us in shared spiritual experiences. Spirituality, an intangible essence, necessitates sharing experiences with others to validate the normalcy and significance of our faith journey. This mutual support is crucial for navigating the path of faith.

The relationships formed within these communities challenge our capacity for love. Initially, our experiences in these communities can be confusing, offering support, acceptance, and judgment. It quickly becomes apparent that faith community members are a mix of flaws and good intentions, often failing to embody the ideals they profess. The existence of a perfect faith community would be concerning, as imperfection is inherent to any group of individuals. While non-faith-based communities often harmonize better due to shared interests and personal motivations, faith communities are expected to outperform these by embodying love, selflessness, and maturity. Yet, disappointment often arises due to the questionable behaviors within these communities.

So, why should we commit to a faith community despite these challenges? There are two compelling reasons:

Firstly, a faith community acts as a spiritual family where members, new and seasoned in their faith journey, support each other. This support system, albeit imperfect, is driven by a divine purpose, allowing us to navigate the complexities and imperfections of communal faith life. Within these imperfections, we explore the divine's presence among us, fostering an understanding and acceptance of human fallibility, including our own, which in turn highlights the essence of grace.

Secondly, being part of a faith community enhances our capacity to love. True love extends beyond fleeting emotions to embrace a timeless and ethereal nature. While it is easy to love those lovable, the actual test of love is our ability to love those deemed unlovable. Such an endeavor requires divine intervention, as only a divinely inspired will can motivate us to extend love unconditionally. Therefore, this journey within a faith community is about seeking or providing support and evolving our understanding and practice of love.

We also need a community centered around mental health professionals that ideally combines faith and mental health. Such a community is crucial for similar reasons to why we value faith communities: they provide a space where we can communicate in a common language and offer mutual support. Within this community, individuals with more outstanding professional and life experience can impart their knowledge and wisdom. Meanwhile, those newer to the field can invigorate the more seasoned professionals with fresh ideas and the latest developments in mental health. This dynamic exchange ensures that everyone can grow and benefit from being part of this community.

Invest in the Lives of Others

As mental health professionals within faith communities, we are deeply committed to supporting struggling individuals. Our role often transcends mere counseling; we become a source of divine guidance for those who have yet to tune into their spiritual senses and a beacon of hope for those who are spiritually seeking but may feel lost. We may find ourselves drawn to specific individuals, and this attraction is often reciprocated, rooted in a shared spirituality. These connections develop naturally, driven by a mutual pursuit of deeper spiritual understanding.

When you find that you have a more spiritual experience and the other person is eager to delve into the deeper aspects of life, showing a willingness to learn and grow, you might be divinely chosen to guide them through their spiritual journey. Being a mentor in faith is an integral part of our own spiritual self-care. Sharing the insights and wisdom we have gained benefits others, rejuvenates our faith, and brings us immeasurable joy, especially when we witness the spiritual growth of those we mentor. This mentorship is a selfless endeavor, yet the spiritual fulfillment we gain from seeing someone else progress in their healing and faith journey is profoundly rewarding.

However, it is important to acknowledge that we may only sometimes see the immediate outcomes of our efforts. By letting go of our attachment to the results, we can truly cherish the loving relationship that develops from our initial role as givers. These mentor-mentee dynamics seldom remain one-sided; instead, they evolve into mutually enriching relationships filled with love and shared spiritual growth.

While the suggestions offer valuable guidelines, it is important to note that they do not encompass the full scope of spiritual care. To effectively integrate these suggested spiritual self-care practices into your life, it is recommended that you blend them gradually with your current habits. By making these practices a natural part of your daily routine, you can introduce additional ones. Being deliberate about your practices is essential to keeping your passion and love alive joyfully offering services to others.

Conclusion

Mental health within faith communities has traditionally faced suspicion and stigma. Yet, this perception is slowly shifting, although some high-level religious leaders remain cautious about fully endorsing mental health care. Despite such hesitancy, the contributions of mental health workers to faith communities are profoundly valuable, often surpassing expectations. This chapter delves into the intrinsic connection between spirituality and mental health, highlighting the importance of approaching individuals from faith communities with an understanding that nurtures healing and growth in their spiritual journey.

In faith-based mental health, caregivers serve as a vital bridge between spirituality and mental well-being. This role demands significant introspection and self-care, which are pivotal to spiritual and mental health. The chapter explores the role of humility in our approach, the influence of different worldviews on our thoughts, emotions, behaviors, and motivations, and the exploration of these motivations. Furthermore, we detail nine spiritual self-care practices essential for caregivers. These practices enable us to sustain our well-being, ensuring we can effectively assist others through life's challenges and continue our vital work in the intersecting fields of spiritual and mental health care.

SHINE Framework

Throughout the chapter, we stress the necessity of a comprehensive approach that blends psychological and spiritual principles for self-care and serving others within faith-based contexts.

SHINE: Spirituality and Health Integration for Nurturing Empowerment

This acronym encapsulates the core message of integrating spirituality and mental health while emphasizing this approach's empowering and uplifting nature. Here's the breakdown of the framework:

Self-Awareness and Spiritual Growth

This component emphasizes the importance of self-reflection, understanding one's worldview, and continuous spiritual development. It relates to the discussion on crafting a personal mission statement, knowing one's religious beliefs, and practicing presence. It encourages mental health professionals to engage in their own spiritual journey to serve others better.

Holistic Healing Approach

This element highlights the text's emphasis on addressing the whole person - spiritual, emotional, relational, and physical. It encompasses the idea that mental health and spirituality are profoundly interconnected and should be treated as such. This approach allows for a more comprehensive understanding of an individual's well-being.

Integration of Faith and Psychology

This component addresses the core slogan and the central theme. It emphasizes the need to blend psychological principles with spiritual practices, as demonstrated in the nine spiritual self-care practices outlined in the chapter. This integration allows for a more nuanced and practical approach to mental health care in faith communities.

Nurturing Communities of Support

This element emphasizes being involved with a faith community and investing in the lives of others. It highlights the importance of creating supportive environments for addressing spiritual and mental health needs. These needs include fostering relationships within faith communities and among mental health professionals.

Empathetic Care and Connection

This final component emphasizes the compassionate and understanding approach needed when working in faith communities. It relates to the discussion on humility, listening to others' stories, and providing care that respects psychological and spiritual dimensions. It also encompasses the idea of connecting with others on a deeper level, as mentioned in the mentorship section of the chapter.

This SHINE framework encapsulates the key themes from the text while providing an actionable and memorable structure for mental health professionals working in faith communities. It emphasizes the integration of spirituality and mental health, aligning closely with the central theme and the overall message.

Jessica H. Leigh, LCSW

Jessica Leigh's inspiring journey in mental health began in a nursing home, where her daily interactions with older adults sparked a deep curiosity about their unique responses to their surroundings. This experience highlighted for her the intricate process of discovering what constitutes a satisfying life.

With a Master's degree in Social Work from the University of Illinois at Chicago, Jessica embarked on a fulfilling role as an early childhood social worker within the Chicago Public Schools. Here, she gained invaluable insights into child development and honed her interest in the evolution of spirituality over time.

Her path then led her to a rewarding position as a counselor and director of women's ministries at a church. In this role, Jessica passionately nurtured the idea of spiritual development, empowering individuals to grow in their faith and navigate life's challenges through effective counseling and training for women's group leaders.

Jessica's adventure continued with Youth With A Mission (YWAM) / the University of the Nations in Kona, where she served as a counselor and educator. Working with missionaries from diverse backgrounds enriched her understanding of how cultural perspectives influence personal growth. She guided countless individuals in exploring their beliefs and motivations on their faith journeys.

Driven by a heartfelt desire to help others discover meaning and purpose, Jessica Leigh is wholeheartedly dedicated to supporting individuals in embracing their true selves and savoring every moment life offers!

Questions for Reflection and Discussion

How can leaders cultivate a trauma-compassionate approach in environments where systemic inequities persist? Reflect on what specific actions leaders can take to ensure people of color feel supported, valued, and seen, beyond just addressing their productivity.

In what ways does the concept of 'person in environment' apply to both educational and workplace settings, and how can this perspective shift how we approach leadership?

Consider how understanding someone's environment, including historical and systemic challenges, can shape more empathetic leadership practices.

What strategies can organizations implement to dismantle the silent strain that microaggressions and systemic inequities place on employees of color?

Discuss practical ways to address the invisible struggles faced by marginalized groups, particularly in predominantly white or male-dominated workplaces.

_____

_____

_____

_____

_____

_____

_____

Reflect on the role of vulnerability in leadership. How can leaders balance transparency about personal struggles with maintaining professional authority? Explore how sharing personal hardships, as described in the passage, can foster stronger relationships and create more empathetic leadership while maintaining credibility.

How can mental health professionals and leaders collaborate to address the compounded trauma that people of color experience in the workplace, and what are the best methods for providing support? Discuss ways to bridge the gap between leadership and mental health resources to create a more holistic support system for employees facing trauma in professional settings.

www.ingramcontent.com/pod-product-compliance
Lightning Source LLC
Chambersburg PA
CBHW061747120626
46550CB00005B/1917